P9-CFW-427

JEFFERSON COLLEGE
3 6021 00019 5010

THE PROFANE COMEDY

THE MACMILLAN COMPANY
NEW YORK • CHICAGO
DALLAS • ATLANTA • SAN FRANCISCO
LONDON • MANILA
IN CANADA
BRETT-MACMILLAN LTD.
GALT, ONTARIO

The Profane Comedy

American Higher Education in the Sixties

KENNETH E. EBLE

New York
THE MACMILLAN COMPANY
1963
A DIVISION OF THE CROWELL-COLLIER PUBLISHING COMPANY

Second Printing 1963

The Macmillan Company, New York
Brett-Macmillan Ltd., Galt, Ontario

Printed in the United States of America

Library of Congress catalog card number: 62-11360

To My Family and Friends

PREFACE

This book assumes that there is something of value which can be said by one man of limited experience about a world as large and complex as the American academic world. The book is only in part personal; frequently I have tried to bring facts into relation with personal assessments. Yet, any book worth writing about American education must be personal; it must not submit to American education's subservience to the chart, the compilation, the continuing study. It must frankly admit that however clear the glass through which one looks, what is seen and written about depends on the eyes and mind and hands that perform the task.

The focus of the book is on higher education. That higher education, and secondary education, and elementary education, and adult education, and, for that matter, "education" are all separate entities is a condition which I'm forced to accept, though not to desire. Arrogance may explain my presuming to knowledge about higher education; ignorance certainly explains my exclusion of that which precedes and follows life on the campus. My view of the campus is that of a student and teacher, though this is an acknowledgment of point of view, not of special knowledge. That the book should be both affectionate and caustic is, I hope, as much because of the character of the academic world as because of the peculiarity of one member of it.

Throughout the book, I refer to those many institutions which make up higher education as *colleges*, *universities*, and *schools*, without a finicky regard for exactness. The alternative was to use the long phrase, *colleges and universities*, each time both were meant. When I specifically mean *college* or *university*, I try to make the context support the use of the term. For the most part, any one of the three terms means the degree-granting institutions of higher education as distinct from a growing number of institutions which give training beyond the high school but which do not grant degrees.

In choosing the title, *The Profane Comedy*, I have weighed the risk of being thought disrespectful to Dante's masterpiece against the advantage of saying much in a short space. American colleges and universities are certainly *profane*, as contrasted with *divine*, and *comedy*, as Dante explained in a letter to Can Grande della Scala, is appropriate to a narrative which begins harshly and ends happily. Any account, however harsh, of an institution so vigorous, so confident, so alive with the promise of youth, as American higher education, must end happily. That the title of this book has other implications makes it no less appropriate to the subject.

ACKNOWLEDGMENTS

I owe much to many individuals for the completion of this book. Since this is a book about college teachers and scholars, I begin by acknowledging my general debt to the three scholar-teachers in whose classrooms I became most aware of the virtues of study and the pleasures of learning: Gerald Else, Victor Harris, and Gilbert Highet. My general thanks, also, to the many teachers and students who have had a part in shaping my vision of the academic world, and to the University of Utah, which has afforded a congenial and stimulating academic climate. Specifically, my thanks to all members of the English department at the University of Utah and to the former head of the department, Edwin Clapp. My special thanks to Don Walker, Jack Adamson, and Milton Voigt, who read the manuscript and made many valuable suggestions, and to Robert and Mary Schaaf, who performed the great service of seeing the manuscript through discerning and nonacademic eyes. My thanks to others with whom I have talked about the book or who have read parts of the manuscript: Robert Helbling, Don Heiney, Hal Moore, Dorothy Snow, Ralph Salisbury, and Martin Zober. My typist, Mrs. Helen Winn, and our departmental secretary, Mrs. Sally Allen, have been of great help.

I wish to thank also the *AAUP Bulletin* for permission to quote from Lloyd Williams's article (Winter, 1957) and from the Association's report on the University of Nevada; *The Journal of Higher Education* for permission to use material that appeared there in a somewhat different form as "The Burden of Bonehead," Vol. XXVIII, January, 1957, pp. 30–37; Erik Wensberg and the *Columbia University Forum* for material that first appeared there as "Head, Heart, and Hand Outstretched," Vol. III, Fall, 1960, pp. 11–15; and Peter Ritner, my editor at Macmillan.

Finally, my greatest thanks to my wife, who performed the greatest service, not only in reading and criticizing the manuscript but in providing both time and encouragement. All of these helped make the book possible; for what is in it, I will have to take the responsibility.

KENNETH EBLE
Salt Lake City, Utah
January, 1962

CONTENTS

THE PROFANE COMEDY

INTRODUCTION

Higher education is a dreary subject. Dealing in large part with the dead, it lacks the vigor of the Board of Trade or the stadium. Being somewhat alive, it lacks the charm of fossils. Yet, the college and the university are largely responsible for the existence of our technological society, and, to a great degree, define our culture.[1]

There is little need to document the intimate relation between science, pure and applied, and the universities. Our two great current concerns, national defense and space research, would collapse if university personnel and university-trained personnel were suddenly to disappear. Business, constantly adapting scientific methods and machinery to its uses, would hardly suffer less. The American household would, sooner or later, be deprived of wonders comparable to today's electric can opener and no-iron fabrics.

The colleges and universities are of equal importance to another part of our existence, that part not directly concerned with physical well-being, with the mere acquisition and consumption of goods. Outside the great metropolitan areas, the colleges and universities are almost the only active centers for the theater, for music, for painting and sculpture, for the reading and writing of books, and for the myriad activities of the mind which loosely comprise "culture."[2] More than that, the college graduate becomes the consumer of culture and oftentimes the missionary for it in the urban and rural areas which are finding the arts almost as interesting as midget auto racing. That the public tacitly recognizes the importance of the college and university is obvious from the fervor which animates people of almost every age and aptitude to pursue a college degree.

Education has a distressing way of plodding off into statistics. That's part of its dreariness. Nevertheless, a few figures need to be introduced here. In 1900, only 4 per cent of the college-age population (18–21) went to college. Today, about one-fourth of the college-age population (18–24) attends,[3] and in the next decade the proportion is certain to go higher.[4] In the state of Utah, which leads the nation in this respect, 1 of every 33 of its population in 1949–1950 was a college student.[5] In the four counties in which the state's major universities are located, more than two-thirds of the high school graduates are now going on to college.[6]

The Office of Education Directory for 1960–1961 lists about 1400 colleges and universities which grant the Bachelor's or the first professional degree, and about 600 junior colleges, technical institutes, and normal schools which give education beyond the twelfth grade.[7]

In size, American institutions which grant college degrees range from the University of California with its 54,000 students on seven scattered campuses to several hundred schools with enrollments of less than 500 each. The nine largest institutions have about 9 per cent of the total enrollment. Manner of support varies widely, too. Though there are almost three times as many privately supported four-year institutions as publicly supported ones, over half of the students are enrolled in public institutions.[8] The majority of private schools are supported by various denominations. Protestant churches support about 500 colleges; the Roman Catholic Church about 300. The liberal arts college is the most typical kind of college. In 1955–1956, there were 650 privately controlled liberal arts colleges and 82 public ones. Together with colleges and universities which offer liberal arts as a basic part of the curriculum, these institutions enroll five-sixths of all resident college students.

American colleges and universities exist in such variety that classifying them gives only a hazy idea of the nature of any individual college. The only really clear distinction is that between coed colleges and those restricted to either sex. In number, men's colleges barely exceed women's colleges, 193 to 189, but the 1053 coed colleges clearly show the American preference.

This excursion into facts and figures discloses a system of higher education that is vast and diverse, and in which the extremes are far apart. The idea for this book grew out of my experiences at a number of quite different institutions. In order, over a period of fifteen years, I was a student, a student and teacher, and finally a teacher, at two large state universities, a very small rural private college, a very large Ivy League graduate school, a medium-sized urban private university, and a somewhat larger state university. These particulars are not put down as a confession nor as a claim to extraordinary experience. Many individuals have had a more varied academic career. Mine was sufficiently varied to force me to see higher education in its diversity as in its sameness. Eventually, it led me to regard the academic world as a cosmos existing at the three levels described in this book: limbo, purgatory, and paradise.

The great number, the variety, and the breadth of services performed are the foremost characteristics of American higher education.[9] Universities, with their ambitious attempts to provide for the study of all knowledge, have always been large in scope. As American colleges became universities, they not only met this traditional obligation but assumed the responsibility for civilizing and socializing a growing proportion of American youth. The two broad courses open to American higher education are described by Robin Williams, Jr.:

> An education system may follow the "Jeffersonian" model—it may open the race to everyone but eliminate all but the best from the final heats; or it may adopt the "Jacksonian" system and provide education

at all levels for anyone. Recent trends in American education apparently have been mainly "Jacksonian." [10]

The debate between "educating" and "civilizing," as it might be called, continues to engage both the public and the academic community. Should the university chiefly aim to develop a high degree of disciplined intelligence in those students capable of such growth, or should it concern itself primarily with developing the general capacities of every citizen?

Perhaps because both goals have much to recommend them, the American university has typically compromised. Though it has not realized the high aims set forth in Newman's *The Idea of a University*, it has clearly embraced this one of his views: "It is a great point then to enlarge the range of studies which a University professes, even for the sake of the students; and, though they cannot pursue every subject which is open to them, they will be the gainers by living among those and under those who represent the whole circle." [11] The awakening experience that higher education provides, an experience open to dull and bright alike, may be the most permanent and consequential effect of going to college. An undergraduate learns little enough in four years, but he has had the sense of what man has done, what he can do. More than that, he has had the close association with other youths whose ideals have not yet succumbed to experience, age, or resignation. Even when, by academic standards, college life becomes most trivial, it is an attractive life and beneficial because it may give the sojourner a vision of a life lived for more than mere acquisition and expenditure.

On the other hand, the traditional sustaining idea behind liberal education has always been, as Cardinal Newman phrased it, "simply the cultivation of the intellect, as such, and its object is nothing more or less than intellectual excellence." [12] Such an idea runs contrary to the beliefs of Jacksonian democracy and arouses the suspicions of those who resent any implications of superiority. Nevertheless, the idea has never been abandoned, and even in universities whose daily routines are devoid of intellect, sentiments favoring intellectual excellence are routinely avowed. Colleges and universities are selective, if not in their students, then in their faculties, and the insistence upon intellectual excellence by the faculty has kept many universities from becoming overpoweringly hostile to the mind.

The American university is much more the world than the European university and it suffers correspondingly from the things of the world. The American emphasis upon things rather than ideas, upon consumption rather than conservation, upon size rather than quality are directly reflected in the universities. They swarm with enterprisers, and scholarship itself is often conducted in the manner of business enterprise. The great achievement of American higher education may be one of logistics. Quality aside, it has developed ways to get large numbers registered, marked, and certified, and has made it possible for a man to pack up his accomplishments at one station and have them shipped to almost any other station down the line.

The students streaming into the colleges and universities cannot be expected to bring much enthusiasm for the academic life with them. An administration concerned with management and public relations is not likely to show continuing devotion to intellectual excellence. That leaves the intellectual character of a university in the hands of the faculty. To me, as an observer and as a faculty member, the professors have not defended the virtues of the intellectual life very well. They have failed to stand as a profession for the ideals which, as individuals, they so solemnly preach. They have let themselves become disengaged from the defining of policies and the defending of principles which should guide a university's life, and have been forced to accept practices which plague their lives. They have, most of all, failed to provide leadership and have frequently excused their failure by conjuring up an impossible public, or an equally impossible administration, tyrannizing over them.

The students and the public and the administration are not free from blame. The students and the public have expected too much and given too little. They have continually taken advantage of natures that are more charitable and democratic sentiments which are more discerning than their own. The best administrations have given higher education the kind of active leadership which conflicting faculty obligations have made difficult for even the best faculty to provide. The worst administrations have left the scholars bent over their books and have erected ramshackle educational structures on their backs.

Higher education has been extremely successful in stimulating criticisms of its own practices, particularly from those who are enmeshed in university routine daily. The criticisms in this book will go to rest with the others before them and the ones to come. Institutions always decline into heaviness, formalism, and vain show. People are always too ignorant, too weak, and too venal. Ideas are always harder to grasp than things, difficult to hold when grasped, tricky, deluding, and troublesome. Money is always hard to come by, and its absence as nourishing to evil as its presence. That higher education at any time should respond magnificently to criticism is more than can be expected. There does seem to be one large gain which suggests that the criticisms of the past have had an effect upon a part of higher education today. The top level now includes more institutions, and many of these are suffering, in David Riesman's phrase, the "stalemate of success."[13] For the majority of institutions, however, the persistence of the critics and the sameness of the criticism testify to the need for all of them to be regularly called to virtue.

What happens to the colleges and universities in the sixties will largely be the consequences of their attempt to educate more students and to give some students a better education. This has been the central problem of higher education throughout the century. The renewed emphasis grows out of the great number of children now in the lower schools, the increased desire to go on to college, and the events in the world which have underlined Alfred North Whitehead's solemn judgment: "In the conditions of modern life the rule is absolute, the race which does not value trained intelligence is doomed." [14]

PART ONE

The Cosmos

1. Limbo

EVEN in a shabby college, the freshmen enrolling probably think their school is one of the greater heavenly bodies. Many of them will never give up this idea and it will bring them back to the campus, at least as far as the stadium, year after year. Professors, who share some of these feelings toward their undergraduate colleges, see a larger part of the cosmos. A majority will have finished graduate work in one of the more glorious graduate schools. Since there are few of these and many obscure colleges, the journey of the new professor from scholar to pedagogue is likely to seem downhill. However fond the undergraduate may be of the college he is attending, the fledgling professor who has descended there from a loftier perch may feel that he is dwelling in an inferior world.

The lowest level of American colleges comprises a kind of Limbo where the educational vagrants, the intellectual pagans, the good but academically unsanctified are assigned. Most of its inhabitants feel grateful for being spared the extreme tortures life can inflict; few escape a continual longing to be somewhere else. Faculty members in Limbo tend to drift from one dismal college to another. A few in each institution become permanent residents. Many last two or three years before moving on. Teachers whose contracts are not renewed at one school arrive at another somewhat down the scale. Others, whose professional competence is not questioned but who have remained long enough to have forsaken scholarship, neglected professional responsibilities, and developed animosities to their surroundings, drift to similar schools, slightly worse or slightly better. Some rise out of Limbo; some remain, cherishing a vision of Paradise; many drift, losing sight of Heaven and becoming inured to Hell.

Such schools exist. They have names like Upper Idaho University, Susan More Hopewell College, Pine City Teachers College. One was brilliantly described under the fictitious name of Cherokee College by Professor Lloyd Williams in the *AAUP Bulletin*. Teachers at dozens of small schools identified it as their own. Professor Williams' concluding diagnosis is harsh but fair:

> Psychologically, Cherokee is sick. The most noticeable consequences stemming from the present ethos and social structure of the College are frustration, emotional insecurity, anxiety, latent and manifest hostility, disguised and undisguised aggression, in conjunction with both self-effacing and self-depreciating tendencies on the part of many. . . . In many respects this College is probably not unlike scores of other colleges across the United States. It is this probability of typicalness that is especially disturbing, for it is a measure of the extent to which authoritarianism, anti-intellectualism, formalism, and irrelevance have captured American higher education.[1]

In part these colleges exist because education and morality have a long history as complementary concerns.[2] Poverty has often completed the trinity. These colleges, usually small ones, located in areas where small towns dot the countryside, have little money with which to compete with larger, better-endowed or state-supported schools. Faculties are secured at the lowest possible rates, and incompetence is tolerated to a higher degree than is consistent with high standards. Their educational philosophy is one which permits piety, loyalty, and devotion to substitute for intellectual effort, discipline, and accomplishment. They tend to drive out the young and keep the old. At the heart of many of them, there lurks the suspicion that the intellect is inevitably corrupting.

These schools have a considerable effect upon the profession. They are often the starting points for college teachers, particularly in times when teachers are not in demand. The impression one gets from beginning here is lasting, and the view of one's chosen profession from this perspective is disheartening. Most members of the faculties of such schools are handicapped in one way or another from achieving high professional competence. The men tend to be conservative, sometimes embittered or warped for various reasons, often compulsively gregarious, or withdrawn into ineffectuality. The women, and they comprise a large portion of these faculties, are likely to be genteel, quiescent, and not up to the rigors of the Ph.D. The administration is usually pious, hidebound, and without intellectual interests. The atmosphere is student-oriented, close in manners and morality, quiet to the point of dullness, and intellectually soporific. The library, compared with even modest public libraries, will be inadequate; the students of real promise few in number; the campus lovely but touched by decay.[3] The central weakness of these colleges is politely touched upon in a student's letter to a national church magazine:

> The church-related college is generally small: a homogeneous community which has many advantages over a large university campus. That community must never forget, however, the dangerous tendency it has to develop an atmosphere of spiritual and intellectual provincialism.[4]

Few of these schools maintain chapters of professional organizations; few of the faculty members attend professional meetings;

few professors have pushed much beyond their field of specialization as it was constituted at the time of their graduate work. Any discussion which attempts to define college teaching as a profession must take into account this group, a group which contributes relatively little to the profession, a group which under better conditions might contribute much more, a group which exists at the low end of the salary scale and may not have a very strong argument for rising higher. A surprising number have met the minimum professional requirement, the Ph.D. degree; indeed, the paltriest schools insist upon it. But the difference between such degree holders and their counterparts in the better universities is probably greater than that between a mediocre rural doctor and a thoroughly competent specialist.

Institutional existence in these Limbo colleges is most often linked with administrative existence. The presidents of such institutions tend to treat these schools as personal properties. As a consequence, the peculiarities of the president are reflected in the institution to a greater degree than elsewhere. Presidents are seldom chosen for their academic distinction; they gain the office by their orthodoxy and their rightness for the community. These colleges are governed by administrations torn between professions of democratic faith and monarchical practices. Autocracy is the prevailing pattern. How personal, yet tangible, a thing the small college presidency can be is illustrated by the recent troubles of Monmouth College, New Jersey.[5] They began when the college acquired an estate in return for making the donor president for a year and president emeritus thereafter, thus creating two heads for one suffering body. Among other vexations, the faculty was plagued with the continual changing of the locks to keep the president emeritus from assuming what he felt were the powers of his office.

The academic dean is next in power to the president. Often a graduate of a teachers college, he is probably more interested in the public schools than in higher education. He brings to his office the heaviness, the respect for authority, the blindness or hostility to intellectual life which graduate work in education and subservience to a conservative public seem to instill. Though he should be the intellectual leader, he is more often the coordinator of committees and schedules, and hardly distinguishable from the registrar and the head of public relations, the next two most important administrative officers. All three have expended much of their energy in the past in ceaseless and profitless recruiting, "beating the bushes" for students. At present, when students are more plentiful, the zeal goes into trying to create an image of academic respectability.

Beyond recruiting, the administration's chief concern is accreditation.[6] Loss of accreditation is fatal to the small, insecure college. Remaining accredited is easier than trying to regain accreditation once lost. A constant attention to the apparent signs of academic excellence keeps the administration busy. Bookkeeping must be orderly, catalogues designed to show both depth and breadth in the program, an impressive number of Ph.D.'s put on the staff. Accreditation varies somewhat from one accrediting agency to another. If their requirement were really insisted upon, few of these colleges would be or would remain accredited. As it is, the voluminous check lists which the colleges fill out, the one-day or two-day visits of accrediting teams, disclose little that the administration does not want to disclose. Like students passing a machine-scored examination, the colleges get by on their familiarity with the mechanics of testing rather than on their proof of excellence.

Life for faculty members who stay on in these colleges becomes more and more identified with institutional life. The old guard, a part of all of these schools, though it may include a frustrated cynic, puts the school first and all else, even personal fulfillment, second. This brings out one's selfless nobility, but it also props up institutions which might better have tumbled. Seldom has any influx of new teachers changed the basic patterns of the past. The appearance of large numbers of veterans as students after the war did change the social and moral climate temporarily. Smoking appeared, and chapel became assembly, and dancing was permitted in the afternoons under supervision. The mild upheaval of the postwar years has now spent itself, and there is little that can be counted on to promote change in the next generation.

The resistance to change is part of the loyalty to alma mater which is almost a contractual obligation of faculty members. Rural people in any part of the country find it difficult to avoid contact with a wider, wickeder, outside world. It is particularly difficult for the faculty of these colleges to remain unaware of the larger academic community. The scattered parts of the academic world are diverse but also pulled toward uniformity. Textbooks adopted by backwater colleges may be ones used in major universities. Professional titles and routines are the same one place as another. Students feel themselves linked with campus fads that make the pages of national magazines. But the line of vision to the outside is obscured by the haze which attraction to the past, loyalty to the present, and grudging acceptance of the future create on the small college campus. The result is often feelings of inferiority which show themselves in resentment toward "attacks" on the college, or in self-effacement before the jargon of pedagogy, or in a suspension of the critical faculty.

The picture drawn is a depressing one. Nowhere else in the educational structure, including the comprehensive high school, is mediocrity so tolerated and is the mixture of morals, abilities, discipline, professions, and practices more unhappy. It is difficult to choose who deserve the most praise: the thousands of dedicated individuals who keep these colleges alive, or those who have refused to serve and so have helped in their demise. In 1900, President Harper of the University of Chicago estimated that one-fourth of America's colleges were doing work of the caliber of the high school or academy.[7] The situation has changed little. The colleges of Limbo are strong contributors to that weakening of educational values which has become the shame of the public schools in the past twenty-five years.

How many and which colleges belong in Limbo is highly speculative. No college is going to admit readily that it belongs there, and any individual who assigns colleges to such a place risks his own damnation. The Office of Education Directory for 1958–1959 lists about 300 degree-granting colleges with student bodies under 500. Most of these are supported by religious groups; some 90 are Roman Catholic institutions staffed by those in orders. By 1960–1961, this figure has dropped to about 265. General enrollment increases have pushed many schools past the 500 mark; a half-dozen colleges have stopped granting degrees or have closed down; about ten began to grant degrees for the first time. In both years, about one-third of the schools are unaccredited or partially accredited. Of the rest, a dozen or so can be called first-rate colleges; the others, measured against any central image of what a liberal arts college should be, are substandard.

Defining the colleges of Limbo as those with fewer than 500 students is arbitrary and misses a good many larger schools no better, or worse, than these small ones. Size, however, does have an effect upon quality. A physical plant and administrative structure need to be of a certain size for a few students as for many; a good library is essential, whether for 200 students or 20,000; laboratories are likewise essential. In a college which attempts a diversified program, a faculty must be of a certain minimum size to make it possible to offer majors in the wide number of studies associated with a liberal arts program. One of Dr. Conant's recommendations for the high schools, whose kind of training is much more compatible with small size, was to increase their enrollments to ensure a minimum of 100 in a graduating class.[8]

Many of these colleges came into existence in the fervor of expansion of religious education in the nineteenth century. During the period 1860 to 1890, 134 new colleges were founded, most of them denominational.[9] Though enrollment in each of these colleges was small, the total enrollment in all colleges and universities increased from 56,286 in 1870 to 156,756 in 1890. By 1910, it was 355,213. Today it is almost 4,000,000. The ratio of students to college-age population has also grown. Before 1890, fewer than 2 out of 100 youths 18 to 24 were attending college. By 1920, this number had risen to 4.46; by 1940, to 9.09. It now stands at about 23.[10]

Paradoxically, the presence of small colleges does little to account for the rapid growth in number of college students at the present time. Proximity undoubtedly stimulates college attendance, and the founders of the small colleges did not need a very large virgin territory to stake out a college. Within 100 miles of Topeka, Kansas, thirty years ago, there were 14 colleges, all of them, Burges Johnson pointed out, engaged in a reckless competition for students.[11] Such competition has not disappeared, but it has changed its character. Now, the small colleges as a group face the urbanization of every state and the compelling pull of the large municipal or state universities. The attractiveness of the small school often lovingly described in reminiscences about college days is somewhat lost on college youth today. The city promises jobs, diversion, excitement, and status. Its enticements are constantly present, through movies, television, and the commonplace experience of driving into the city for a night of fun. Rural life has suffered and so have the colleges which were founded to make it easy for rural youth to gain an education.

The state of Iowa gives a kind of average picture of the presence and plight of the small colleges. In the proportion of a state's population attending college, Iowa is almost exactly in the middle.[12] About 25 per cent of its youth attends college, and most of these choose institutions within the state. Like the rest of the

Midwest, Iowa was affected by the zeal with which denominations set up colleges almost before they set up the church. Like other states, it has a land-grant school for agriculture as well as a state university. Though the state has never been generous in supporting its state schools, it seems to reflect its early settlers' reliance upon education to meet the challenges of the frontier. As in many other states, its small towns and rural areas are being depleted as the concentration of population moves toward urban centers.

Its private colleges are numerous; most of them fall into Limbo. In the northeast section, within a circle 100 miles in diameter, there are Wartburg, Luther, Clarke, University of Dubuque, Loras, Upper Iowa University, Cornell, Coe, Iowa State Teachers College, and a spattering of junior colleges. Just outside the periphery of this circle are the State University of Iowa to the south, Iowa State University to the southwest. Except for the southwest part of the state, the other areas show similar developments. In Iowa's colleges, one can read the pattern of migration and settlement, from the Catholic colleges along the Mississippi, to the Lutheran schools of the north, to the Dutch Reformed College at Pella. In the Iowa of today, many of them are charming. Almost all are anachronistic.

They form conferences, play football and basketball, hold debates, publish yearbooks, hold alumni reunions, put students through four years, and constantly want for financial security. All of them resist change, fight against oblivion, and oppose relocation in larger communities which might support them more adequately as community colleges. Though some have lost their original denominational ties, their different backgrounds make efforts at consolidation futile. What energy they still possess is largely spent in justifying their existence.

The conditions described have remained much the same since the late nineteenth century. Once founded, a college clings tenaciously to life. Intellectually impoverished as it may be, it can argue its worth not only on the basis of its particular merits but on the general merits that higher education claims. College and university training instills democratic ideals, acquaints the young with the world's great ideas, fosters development of enduring values, develops the individual to his fullest capabilities, provides trained, skilled men and women necessary to a technological society—these are the standard arguments.

In addition, the small college argues for its special merits.[13] It enlarges the student's perspective without taking him out of his home environment; it provides a personal, friendly atmosphere where student and teacher learn together; it preserves and passes on the Christian tradition; it builds character as well as intellect. With these are a number of practical arguments: the small colleges provide places for students; they produce teachers; they provide jobs; they preserve communities which otherwise might die.

The arguments are not very convincing, not convincing enough to excuse the low level at which most of these colleges operate. The defense of institutionalized higher education rests upon the quality of facilities and faculty, and upon the richness of intellectual milieu which the small, impoverished college finds impossible to provide. Worse, the small college, regardless of its deficiencies, models itself after the big college. Its ideals, when phrased, are echoes of Newman's idea of a university put into language that the local Kiwanis Club can understand. Its catalogue displays as many courses as the printing budget will allow, and though this number falls somewhat short of the number offered at a state university, it is certain to include all the gadget courses, all those which have current vogue.

Many of these schools continue to carry the name "university," and practice a deliberate self-deception as ruinous to the faculty and the institution as any other single practice. If the hard-pressed small schools were willing to exercise more independence, were content to narrow their function, were capable of developing a limited curriculum which could be well taught within the limitations of the schools, they might fulfill an educational goal being missed by far more financially secure colleges. And if, as a result of husbanding their resources, they could assemble a faculty devoid of the Ph.D. and other trappings but marked by youthful vigor and intelligence (surely the great number of M.A. candidates could furnish these), they might come reasonably close to being institutions of higher education.

Few are willing to move in these directions. Fewer still are willing to look toward collaboration with other schools, toward pooling of intellectual resources (not merely banding together to apportion wealthy donors), toward fitting themselves into a total effort of higher education in which they might play a smaller but more dignified and more purposeful part.

In most of these schools, the democratic ideal becomes confused with lack of standards, principles, and objectives. Ideas are smothered in platitudes; values are those the student brings with him and which the community has always had. The individual receives, on the one hand, sufficient training for a limited number of jobs (teaching chief among them), and, on the other, puts off the necessity to take a job he could have been ready for four years earlier.

Nor is there any less confusion in the emphasis put upon the building of character. Character building, like moral victory, seems to be the peculiar province of wretched colleges and losing football teams. But surely the forces that build character precede the playing fields of Texas A. & M. If one really believes that a boy or girl of eighteen is chiefly deficient in character training, then the professor might as well close his classroom and go home. A man is more than and greater than a mind, but few individuals, and these would include many who cry loudest for education of *character*, would trust the undisciplined, unknowing intelligence even when united with highly refined sentiments. Nevertheless, the small college, plagued by its inferiorities, develops a compensatory distrust for education which selects students with care and which demands intellectual excellence of them. The defensiveness leads to a distrust of intellect, a disdain for achievement, and a comfort in pious mediocrity. Such a philosophy neglects both discipline and exactness, habits of mind which cannot be neglected if intellect is honored, and as necessary to the moral being as to the intellectual one.

If one were to add to this group of very small colleges, many of the colleges under 1000 students, and then to these, the number of colleges, regardless of size, which have inadequate libraries, meager resources, scanty laboratory equipment, a curriculum which attempts to encompass all knowledge, too many students per faculty member, and a faculty very spotty in quality, the inferno might yawn for half or more of American higher education. A check through the Office of Education survey of library statistics for 1959–1960 reveals that only 300 colleges of the approximately 1400 institutions reporting spent over $50 per student annually for their libraries.[14] By comparison, Harvard spent $314; Oberlin, $103; almost all the state universities, between $50 and $100. Another rough measure is the fact that only 659 of about 1400 degree-granting colleges have campus chapters of the American Association of University Professors. A much smaller number, 173 colleges and universities, have chapters of Phi Beta Kappa. One last measure, that of salaries, shows that 181 out of 448 institutions reporting to the AAUP Committee on the Economic Status of the Profession had minimum salary scales of E or below measured against an AA to G standard.[15] The lower depths, it is certain, shelter too many colleges and universities whose presence should be embarrassing to everyone concerned.

Ultimately, one may decide that even the most inferior college does little harm and may do some good. At the least, it satisfies the desires of some students to go to college. If we suppose that the virtue of any college is the fuller development of the human being for the greater glory of man and God, then even the slightest wavering in these directions is a positive force. The bookkeeping becomes too complex here for exactness. If we assume that the expenditure of spiritual and material energies that go into maintaining these colleges must be subtracted from the total amount that gets spent upon higher education, we may be keeping up an unprofitable investment. We may be paying too much for nostalgia, too much for innocence, too much for vague democracy, too much for education whose aim is not so much development as indiscriminate preservation.

Were these colleges capable of upholding the values they publicly espouse, were these values sound, and were the individual colleges somewhat better than most of them are, these colleges would deserve the efforts now being made to keep them going. As it is, the passing of one or another of them from the Limbo of higher education is no great cause for alarm. New colleges, even small colleges, cannot be established on the basis of earnestness and zeal which brought too many colleges into existence in the past. Existing colleges whose humble beginnings have turned into an indigent old age must look to improvement—by consolidation, by limitation of function, by a strenuous and successful effort to strengthen facilities and faculty—to justify their continuing existence.

What is most pitiful of all about these colleges is that, even when they recognize their deficiencies as four-year colleges, they fall back upon a comfortable assurance that they can at least train teachers for the public schools. As noble as the intention is, its fulfillment contributes to the mediocrity which besets the profession of public school teaching. Since the colleges of Limbo remain equal partners in what passes for four years of higher education, they also contribute to the difficulty of developing a profession of college teaching which has both dignity and strength. The quality of education, whether at the higher or the lower level, ultimately depends upon the quality of the teaching profession.

2. Purgatory

PURGATORY, as it should be in all man-created religions, is the largest part of the academic cosmos.[1] To anyone who has just moved up from Limbo, it may be mistaken at first for Paradise; after a time, such optimists find themselves in harmony with those who began their careers at this level. All alike feel a sense of strain at being pumpers of intellectual gas, caught up in genteel poverty, dogged by departmental feuds, faced with challenges neither they nor the institutions they serve are quite up to. I am leveling out individual distinctions to talk about the bulk of American colleges and universities somewhere between the Limbo just discussed and the handful of first-rate universities of which this country can boast.

As a name for the middle circle, Purgatory fits. More and more young people cannot face the perils of life without college, and for many of these the four years is the necessary period of trial and suffering that prepares them for Paradise. That the trials are not severe, the suffering unapparent, is consonant with the Paradise imagined by these penitents. For most, it is the good job with a good firm with a good wife and good children in a good home in a good community in the best of all possible worlds.[2] The notion that salvation may not lie on the other side of a college education has not yet filtered out into the public, and the middle ground of higher education may be the gathering place for a majority of American citizens within twenty-five years.

For the faculty, Purgatory is not, as it is for the students, a comfort station on the way to Paradise. It is for most a permanent position where one cannot still the yearning for a higher life or for the tranquillity which lingers at the top of Hell. The splendor of the campuses suggests that scholarship is not a foremost concern of these institutions, taken as a group, or for that matter, that they are very interested in developing the student's intellect. It also suggests that bureaucracy and social service are the lot of those faculty members who reach this level of academic life.

What President Coffman of Minnesota said of the state university could be applied to almost all colleges of the middle range: ". . . there is no intellectual service too undignified for them to perform." [3] The statement can be taken as both a compliment and an indictment. Perhaps no more could be expected of a higher education designed to meet the needs of all who enter the doors for whatever reason. If one substitutes "social" for "intellectual," the statement becomes the debilitating principle which dominates American higher education today.[4]

Social service is a worthy ideal, and carried out in particular ways, keeps degenerates off the streets, comforts the aged, supports the indigent, and cements individuals into communities of one kind or another. In the universities, the ideal of social service has resulted in agricultural extension services, contracts for defense and allied research, training for drivers, secretaries, coaches, dancers, acrobats, forgers, embezzlers, movie producers, hair setters, and public relations men.[5] It has provided entertainment for millions, emotional commitments for only a few less, a sense of purpose for some. It has, on the other hand, worked against the development of intellectual excellence, has ministered little to the spirit, and has infected idealism with the germs of continuing progress and material well-being.

Vocationalism, mechanization, and confusion of purpose result from too intense a devotion to the ideals of social service. The marketplace curriculum of a large university is its chief horror. Whatever pieces of knowledge are readily packageable in three-hour units and readily marketable to immature and practically oriented minds are admissable to the university catalogue. Once admitted, one item is just as good as another. Value distinctions must not be made by a faculty locked into a network of divergent interests.

Water Polo, which fulfills a major in a major department, *is* just as important as Greek, which fulfills a major in a department as superior in its intellectual content as it is inferior in number of students. The one, dragging with it a cluster of courses—*Water Safety*, *First Aid*, *Swimming 1*, *2*, *3*, and *4*, *Playground Management*—promises to meet an immediate vocational need as well as a social need in a way that Greek and its cluster of courses—*The Ancient World*, *Thucydides*, *Homer*, *The Pre-Socratic Philosophers*—obviously do not. Were the students in both departments required to submit reasoned briefs for the values of swimming as opposed to Greek literature, both courses might serve worthy purposes. But no student, in either class, is. The one student splashes through his courses in a world which has neither historical nor philosophical dimensions—the other clutches his copy of Pindar as he drowns.

The university catalogue is a fairly accurate index to the country's intellectual history, including its profundities, its fads, and its uneasy tributes to the past. The proliferation of courses is most often blamed upon the desires of narrow specialists and the petty statesmanship of jealous departments. The cause is much more fundamental than that. American colleges have never been ivory tower institutions. They were designed to train graduates for specific purposes, though they followed in the pattern of European universities and taught a limited curriculum designed to instill principles rather than prescribe techniques. Not until the mid-nineteenth century did colleges begin to remodel their offerings to fit the changing needs of the society. Since then, the college curriculum has been steadily expanded to provide courses of training for almost all occupations demanding more than rudimentary skills.

The colleges and universities have become training schools for a great variety of occupations that could be prepared for outside the university at less cost and with greater efficiency. Secretarial training, for example, is a useful pursuit. The academic community would be as lost as the business world if good secretaries were not available. Yet, secretarial training, in itself, can hardly fill four years of academic work. Business colleges manage nicely in two years or two months. The colleges, great fillers of space, do not. Instead, they develop an inflated program of training for secretaries, adding to the difficulties of private institutions specifically designed for that purpose, and detracting from the idea of what a college should be.

Because of its ability to meet every conceivable occupational interest, the college of Purgatory ensures all who arrive that salvation awaits the successful climb onward and upward. Though the high drop-out rate suggests that grace will be denied many, the failure to push on is often one of difficulty in finding the path rather than of being unable to surmount its difficulties. The credit system, which prescribes the way to a bachelor's degree, is as complex, regular, and accessible as the theory of the treasury which prescribed the way to medieval salvation. Indulgences are sold in popular units of 3 hours per semester, and salvation is granted at 128 hours.

It is these universities we can praise and blame for making an education possible for great numbers and for developing the machinery which gives the process an air of efficiency. The credit system, as absurd as that system seems, is largely responsible for the size of the university bureaucracy today. Certainly other means could have been devised to make it possible for multitudes to attend the universities. Few other ways would have sustained the fond American fervor for doing great deeds on a grand scale by means of management and machinery.

The credit system led directly to the efficiency university. Its goal has been that of developing complete confidence in the mechanics of education as education itself. So it is that the small school versus big school controversy takes the form of the personal, humane, individual education versus impersonal, mechanical, mass education. But the small colleges, unfortunately, are as tied to the mechanics of education as the big schools—and with less justification. Wherever an American student goes to college in this country, he is going to spend too much time clambering over the machinery.

Setting up schedules, meeting requirements, transferring credits, withdrawing from classes, paying fees, and the rest, do get in the way of training the mind, except, of course, in these activities. Faced with many students and motivated by an ideal of service to the community, the large university has sought to refine its mechanical services instead of fulfilling its higher aspirations. What prevents it from becoming even more mechanical is the presence within the university of departments and individuals devoted to the traditional ideals of intellectual excellence and the search for truth. Such devotion creates a saving tension between the practical and the ideal.

The practical is upheld by teachers of those subjects which can be adapted easily to the large class, the seating chart, the machine-scored test, the transfer of raw information from pedagogue to pupil by the most efficient means. Teachers like to lecture, and a large audience in a morning class is as gratifying as a full house at a matinee. Social science, history, psychology, education, economics, business, government, political science—these are a few of the courses which can be easily taught to large groups. How well they can be taught is not the question, for the determination of the best way to teach a subject is such a misty conjecture that such speculations have little weight in choosing the pattern of instruction. Teaching more students with fewer faculty is the first principle of efficient academic management.

In the sciences, the nature of laboratory work and the facilities which it requires have made mass instruction difficult. In medicine, similar conditions exist. The medical school's emphasis upon standards, weak in almost every other branch of education, has made classes small, and the quality of instruction correspondingly high. In the humanities, few subjects now escape the demand for efficiency. The two which offer most resistance are mathematics and languages. Teaching courses in these two disciplines to large groups is possible, either with or without television. But, in mathematics, the need for immediate explanation, for questions and answers, for demonstration, militates against very large classes. So does the fact that mastery at one level of mathematics is dependent upon mastery at the previous level. In languages, whether in learning a new tongue or in trying to master one's own, immediate exchange between student and teacher is vital. In English, no way has yet been discovered to lecture literacy into existence.

As a consequence, in the large universities there is a tendency to find departments of language and literature and of mathematics representing a conservative point of view, and the college of education, the social sciences, the college of business, representing the new world of efficiency. Faculty members in the "scholarly" fields are products of conservative graduate schools, specialized to a high degree, and expected to put research first among their duties. Many of the graduate degrees in the other disciplines are granted by universities without a long academic tradition or from a relatively unsanctified program of doctoral study within an established graduate school.

The result is a clash between the ideals of social service and those of a disinterested and sometimes disoriented search for truth. This is a saving conflict if one views the pursuit of truth as the highest business of the university. The university keeps its place in the world even as it surveys the eternities. The ivory tower, a pejorative term in American education, never gets so tall or so white that it arouses the public to destroy it. The balance struck between these opposed ideals seldom results in the harmony which state university presidents like to describe. Having little real respect for scholarship, the schools of Purgatory grudgingly permit it because "research" is the prevailing value in Paradise. Encouraged by the faculty members who were trained in the great research centers, the administrators of middle level universities demand, at all levels of university life, the letter of academic greatness but often overlook the spirit.

As these schools become more impressed with their greatness, research becomes the supreme measure of excellence. The pursuit of truth which research is supposed to entail comes closer to being a sharp eye out for immediate social benefits. The sciences tend to prosper in Purgatory, and the humanities to stimulate impassioned declarations about higher values. The quarrel between science and the humanities never gets resolved, and for that matter, the terms of the quarrel are not very clearly understood. Cooperation between the two becomes even more impossible than the size of the institution makes it.

The humanistic scholars find themselves in an odd position. They waste much time trying to justify their activities as of service to society. They waste even more by aping the research methods, attitudes, even the machines and terminology of the sciences, and occupy themselves with humanistic research which is far from humanistic and dubiously research. Such accomplishments become the measure of a faculty member's excellence. Smaller colleges often are able to measure faculty quality by more than a single standard. The colleges of Purgatory seldom do. The search for truth is a race to get lines in the annual list of faculty publications.

Under the pressure for research, the humanists, by tradition devoted to passing on "humane learning" from one generation to the next, find themselves demanding the right to spend most of their academic lives apart from the students. With the scientists, they become that part of the university which fails to become student-oriented. Thus the intellectual life of the student falls largely into the hands of those dedicated to group dynamics, to cures for juvenile delinquency, and to home decoration. Since the humanists and the scientists have little time for the students and since the social servers have much time for everything but intellectual discipline, the intellectual development of the students is pretty much a by-product of the classroom and quite independent of what the professors may be doing.

Such an education is probably what the modern administrator of a large college in Purgatory has in mind. It deludes the professor into thinking he is doing something worthwhile but not worthwhile enough to demand either respect or money. It processes a great number of students in a fairly short time. As the schools grow larger, more emphasis will be placed upon this kind of efficiency which does not sacrifice appearances. Education conceived of as an art is an inefficient business. Conceived of as social service, it is guilty of misuse of public and private funds if it is not efficient.

The quest for efficiency could lead to a sharper distinction between undergraduate colleges and graduate schools. It might even separate the general undergraduate college from the college which prepares its students for advanced work. Ideally, it might even begin to differentiate between degrees, and thus restore some meaning to both the B.A. degree and the M.A. Schools with great investments in libraries, equipment, and faculty should be able to employ their resources more effectively if they worked with students who had been winnowed by a less costly kind of undergraduate college or specifically prepared for advanced work. In these ways, the demand for efficiency might be turned to good account.

Unfortunately, the colleges and universities of the middle group are not inclined to relate their individual activities to the general needs of higher education. The ambitious schools of this group are bent on moving to higher ground. Even the poorer colleges are unwilling to define their purposes to fit humble goals. Onward and upward for these universities means, first, the granting of the M.A. degree, and then the granting of the Ph.D. Many of the universities of Purgatory will move to the fringes of Paradise, and their faculties will sustain themselves by getting back to the work that their graduate schools prepared them to do. That the graduate pedant they are likely to produce will be markedly superior to the undergraduate numbskull they have left behind is questionable. In Purgatory, indulgences are granted to anyone who pays the price; true salvation comes to very few.

3. *Paradise*

At the highest level of the academic profession are the dozen or so schools which attract faculties with international reputations, pay them well, and enable them to contribute to the intellectual life of the country out of all proportion to their numbers.[1] An increasing number of articles in national magazines bear their authorship. Their books, like David Riesman's *The Lonely Crowd* and John K. Galbraith's *The Affluent Society*, place high on best-seller lists. Their services are frequently requested by industry and government. With the much larger group which comprise a portion of the faculties of many state universities and some large and small private colleges, these college teachers are professional intellectuals.

When the national magazines turn to higher education (and thereby fulfill their college-trained editors' ideas of social service), it is to these colleges that they turn.[2] The colleges and universities which occupy Paradise are roughly those schools known to the general public other than through their football teams.[3] Harvard, Princeton, Yale are still the trinity, and with them

Columbia, the University of Chicago, Johns Hopkins, California and some Big Ten schools. Other colleges, MIT and Cal. Tech. chief among them, are as impressive as these, but have a more restricted function. A scattering of undergraduate liberal arts colleges, like Reed College, Swarthmore, or Oberlin, deserve mention, and many of their graduates will end up in the best graduate schools and become further identified with the highest reaches of higher education. This list is not intended to be precisely inclusive. The focus of attention will be on the handful of universities which maintain undergraduate and graduate schools of distinction and which attempt to embrace all knowledge.

This level of the profession is far removed from Limbo. The teacher who finds himself here, however, has not found beatitude. As an afflicted colleague once pointed out, the "U" of these universities often stands for "ulcer." The professor who arrives here after toiling in lesser vineyards, or the one who was elected as an undergraduate and remains at the price of continually renewing his promise, finds no end to earthly desires. A young professor at Princeton and an alumnus of the graduate school recently expressed his increasing disillusionment with academic life. "Somehow," he wrote, "I had had the impression that the pursuit and teaching of higher learning were a rather dignified business. To my dismay, the pettiness, backbiting and organizational timidity that I encountered turned out to be worse than in any other type of job I had ever held before." [4] Only in a secular Paradise could one find the bitchiness which often marks faculty relationships, the disdain frequently accorded the students, the maneuvering for position and prestige, the grudging acceptance given outsiders, and the mild corruption of human values which power and high position and rare intellect can bring. It is only at this level of university life that professors can truthfully be called "the affluent professors," a journalistic tag given currency by Spencer Klaw in an article in *The Reporter*.[5] The price of affluence, as the article justly pointed out, is often the neglect of or diversion from full participation in university life. In the sciences, this diversion is particularly serious. Were it not for the fact that scientists have gained sufficient prestige and are in sufficient demand to temper the research proposals made by private industry and the federal government, the science faculties of a major university might not be much different from the research departments of any large industry.

Federal and private aid to research is of great importance to these universities, where money is generously awarded for proposals, specific projects, consultation, and even meditation. Even the humanists are under obligation to a number of prominent benefactors. So intense has been the wooing of the professors by gentlemen callers from the world outside that most of the universities of the middle range are similarly affected. A side effect of this demand for the best man or the best team has been the increasing of the distance between Limbo and Paradise. The impoverished of Academia have neither a Unesco, a Ford Foundation, or a Smith-Mundt Exchange program to entice the academic great, either as individuals or as teams. The self-satisfaction and smugness of the saved keep them from worrying about the damned. Perhaps it is fitting that the great universities have become the strongholds of free (but richly endowed) enterprise. A professor does not enter Paradise with a view to leaving the world behind. He enters in order to make the world meet his terms.

For the small-town boy of intellectual promise, Harvard is probably first choice among colleges. He finds it tough to get in, not quite so tough to stay in, and an introduction to a special way of life if he gets in. He automatically moves up into a favored class, a class in which wealth means much. Social position may not make up for intellectual dullness, but neither does it detract from intellectual luster.

Undergraduate life in the schools of Paradise shuts out the world in a way that college life elsewhere does not. There is an aura about being an occupant of one of the houses at Harvard or in joining a club at Princeton which threatens to make the rest of life an epilogue. Unlike the rest of the nation's undergraduates, these precious few are not preparing for life; they have life. In sober fact, their years in college are customarily extended by the years in graduate school. About two-thirds of the students at Harvard go on for advanced study. Vocational courses as such are frowned upon in Harvard College. If one lusts after the market place, he must wait until he can enter the Graduate School of Business.

In this respect, as in others, these schools preserve an honored academic tradition. Four years is a brief enough time, and the ideal of giving youth a period of contemplation, study, and development, freed from the outside world, needs to be defended. Margaret Mead recently wrote:

> The true undergraduate university is still an "as-if" world in which the student need not commit himself yet. For this is a period in which it is possible not only to specialize but to taste, if only for a semester, all the possibilities of scholarship and science, of great commitment, and the special delights to which civilized man has access today.
>
> One of the requirements of such a life has been freedom from responsibility. Founders and administrators of universities have struggled through the years to provide places where young men, and more recently young women, and young men and women together, would be free—in a way they can never be free again—to explore before they settle on the way their lives are to be lived.[6]

College students are favored youth; many feel so favored; a surprising number develop attitudes and values which show that their understanding has broadened and deepened, their judgment sharpened. Among the only heartening conclusions in that disturbing book, *Changing Values in College*, by Philip Jacob, was that a few of the best colleges do something more than merely strengthen the values the student had when he entered college.[7]

What the undergraduate does not leave behind is the intense competition usually associated with the vulgar world. Where the students have been so carefully selected, where the intellectual life is prized, where one deliberately and constantly exposes himself to the measure of historic greatness, such competition may be unavoidable. Competition to get into these schools is fierce, and the selection from a rather narrow range of brilliance makes the desire to excel difficult to satisfy. Since many of these colleges pride themselves on a democratic selection of this intellectual aristocracy, the social and economic differences—family, wealth, community, region—create feelings of inferiority and superiority which can be worked off or strengthened by strenuous intellectual efforts.

For all that, these colleges are not the counseling and guidance centers which many lesser institutions have become. If the students are goaded by a desire to excel, the goals they reach are correspondingly high. Glibness and sharpness, rather than profundity, may mar the intellectual displays put on by the undergraduates. Smugness may detract from their personal attractiveness. A naïveté of experience, socially, emotionally, geographically (sexually, modern writers seem to imply), may set them apart from other bright undergraduates. Yet, when they graduate (and 90 per cent do), they comprise virtually the only group of college graduates in the country in which every member can write reasonably well, think with some precision and some tenacity, and read and have an idea of what is worth reading.

The undergraduate college, however, is not what gives the elite of American universities their national importance. With the exception of a small number of first-rate liberal arts colleges, all of them are known for their graduate schools as much as for their undergraduate colleges. Their special contribution to higher education is in large part the great number of graduate degrees they confer. Over the years, a handful of universities have provided most of the nation's highest degrees.[8] Columbia, Chicago, and Harvard lead in the total number of Ph.D. degrees granted. In recent years, the large number of degrees granted by such state universities as Wisconsin, Illinois, Michigan, and Ohio State have made them as important as the great private universities in this respect. Though about two hundred universities now offer the Ph.D. degrees, academic prestige still depends upon having the degree from one of the prominent universities.

Many of the graduate students in these universities come from the graduate school's undergraduate college. Some, Harvard and Princeton, for example, have a fairly close tie between undergraduate and graduate education. Others, like Columbia, have a more distant relationship. In all the graduate schools, as the student moves closer to the Ph.D. degree, the atmosphere becomes more refined, remote, impersonal, and both scholarly and practical.

The graduate faculties of Paradise are distinguished by specialization, by a stress upon intellectual excellence, by the ideal of greatness, by the facilities for discovering past, present, and future. They set and maintain standards, preserve and create culture, and are, as befits a rich and dominant country, communities of scholars inferior to none. They are also snobbish in the eyes of the rest of the academic world, in much the same way that they themselves feel the superior snobbishness of Oxford or Cambridge. Even among these prominent universities, there are degrees of rank. The higher snobbishness reveals itself in the insistence at Harvard upon calling the professor "Mister," not Doctor or Professor. It also permits the employing of brilliant men, such as the late George Lyman Kittredge, who somehow manage a life of scholarship without the Ph.D. degree.

In many other ways, the graduate schools set a standard of academic living to which the rest of the profession aspires. Salaries are highest, prestige highest. Their presses publish more books and usually better books. Their graduate degrees are often but passing honors on the way to more prominent distinctions. Their endowments and their ability to attract more are the only impressive financial achievements in American education. They attract brilliant faculty and students, sometimes drawing them away from other graduate schools whose needs may be greater but whose attractiveness is less.

As befits temples in Paradise, they shine with the clear light of purest intelligence. Among the many institutions engaged in higher learning, these alone have academic practices which accord very closely with the traditional ideals of education in the Western world. Their main faults are that they are too few, too costly, and too conservative. Perhaps their excellence can be achieved in no other way.

The top level of American universities, measured by number of faculty or number of students, comprises not more than 5 per cent of those engaged in higher education. Using salary as a measure of excellence, we find that in 1960–1961 only four universities in the country were paying an average salary of $11,000 and above. This is a precious portion of the 1400 colleges and universities. Seymour Harris estimated that 13.3 per cent of college faculty members in 1958 received over $10,000.[9] The average income of all self-employed physicians in that year was $16,000.

But this comparison is not designed to bring out the financial plight of the profession. It is designed to raise the general point that academic salaries indicate how small the top of the profession really is. Other measures of academic excellence—quality of teachers and quality of students, for example—would suggest, though less strikingly, a similar conclusion. The difficulty is that measures of academic excellence are hard to find and hard to apply. Without such measures, mapping the area at the top of higher education is a speculative enterprise, at best. The area of excellence is very small if it is restricted only to those schools which maintain a high level of excellence in all aspects of institutional life. It can be expanded considerably by granting the existence of excellence here and there in institutions whose general level is below the top rank.

It is possible, as defenders of American higher education are fond of pointing out, for a gifted student to receive the highest kind of academic training in many colleges and universities. It is also possible for a student, however sluggish, to find some institution which will take him in and nurse him through. It is even possible—in fact very likely—that these two kinds of students will be found in the same institution. This last possibility dictates caution in granting a place at the top to schools afflicted with the common blights which work against over-all excellence.

Few colleges of genuine over-all excellence have been established in the present century. More than fifty colleges and universities (many of them women's colleges and denominational colleges) were established from 1930 to the present. Of these, Wayne State University, Brandeis, Hofstra, and the University of Kansas City can be picked out as having some impetus in the direction of excellence. Only Brandeis appears not to have made a compromise with the ideals of the large, multipurpose universities in which excellence and mediocrity dwell uneasily together. Though there is a persistent tendency on the part of colleges at all levels to aspire to a higher position, that tendency seldom produces a realistic appraisal of the college's ability to get there. The aspirations of existing colleges to move to the topmost rank too often result in merely spreading out a slightly higher level of mediocrity.

Nothing is easier than establishing a college. Establishing a good one is both difficult and costly. Higher education is a costly business. Though family fortunes could and did establish the beginnings of Stanford, Johns Hopkins, and the University of Chicago, few family fortunes of the present day would be adequate to give a new first-rate university a running start. The

$20,000,000 gift to establish Stanford is about the size of the yearly budget of a medium-sized university today. The operating budget of a Harvard or Columbia is the size of a large corporation's. The direct sale of the university's product, however, does not add up to a happy profit. Colleges and universities do result in great profit to the country, but people are less willing to spend money on them than on immediate sensory pleasures. It does not even do much good—except to create an indiscriminate desire for every person to go to college—to point out that the money an individual spends on a college education results in a statistically greater earning power.

To send a boy or girl to one of the country's first-rate private universities costs someone a good deal of money. Tuitions there, about $750 a semester, are now the highest in the country, not only because of their excellence but because the great private universities are more realistic about money than most universities. They have all faced the fact that a first-rate education cannot be provided at a low cost. Though they put a good deal of money into scholarships, they insist that tuition pay a respectable share of the educational expense. The competition for admission to the best private universities may suggest to other private universities that the public will pay the price of a first-class education, even if this price reveals itself in higher tuition fees. How high tuitions can go, even in the very best private universities, is open to question. That they could or should pay the full cost of the student's education (determining this cost becomes very complicated in a first-rate university) is being widely debated right now.

The best universities have also been leaders in responsible financial management of their funds. Current criticism of unwise academic financial policies, ranging from too high a unit cost of production to lack of cost accounting, is much less applicable to the top range of universities than to others. Just as they are more successful in getting money, so are they wiser in spending it. Wise or not, they are able to maintain institutional health by virtue of possessing two vital attributes: long histories which help mightily in the accumulation of endowments and a marked ability to attract large private gifts. Their steady fidelity to excellence has had its pecuniary consequences too. The alumni of the great universities have great individual and aggregate earning power, and have had the kind of experience which leaves them more susceptible to putting some of that money back into the university. Expanding this sector of higher education means a higher per capita investment, either in private gifts or in public funds. Without that, the number of first-rate institutions or first-rate areas within an institution will remain small, the competition for admission into the select schools intense, and the cost to the student, his family, and the institution, high.

Though they set standards for the rest of the nation's colleges and universities, the schools of Paradise do not really lead. The ideals they uphold and which in this way are kept before lesser schools are worthy ones: the disinterested search for truth, the high degree of academic freedom, the respect and opportunities for the faculty, the large number of scholarships, the deemphasis of athletics and extracurricular activities, the maintenance of academic standards, the central position of the library, and the resistance to national fraternity and sorority systems (this last attributable not so much to conviction as to the essential superiority of local campus clubs.) But, though "they do it at Columbia" is still a persuasive argument for the adoption of practices at many colleges, what they do at Columbia is not likely to startle the world by its daring.

The temper of Paradise is conservative.[10] Without discussing the general strengths and weaknesses of the conservative position, one can conjecture that many traditional academic practices have no more warrant for their soundness than traditional political practices. From time to time, strong men with decided opinions—Eliot of Harvard, Hutchins of Chicago—have established new patterns which have the look of reasoned judgments based upon an acute awareness of the past, full cognizance of the present, and anticipation of the future. Where there has been leadership at all, one might claim, it has come from the select schools. But this leadership has been an accidental kind, and it has often had similar consequences. The free elective system was copied by almost all the nation's colleges. The perniciousness of the system has grown through the years at a rate almost directly proportional to the distance of the borrower from the source. Columbia College's Humanities program was similarly copied throughout the country. Such innovations, however, are a long way from consequential and continuing attention to the needs of higher education.

What threatens to happen to higher education has already happened to public education below the college level. The educational policies in the lower schools are not made or even greatly influenced by that tiny area of excellence which still can be found in some public and private secondary schools. Nor, for that matter, do the respectable liberal arts colleges exercise an influence upon the secondary schools to any degree. The major influence is professional "education" as practiced in the catch-all high schools and as professed in the colleges of education. In a similar way, the colleges and universities of real excellence have been almost as unconcerned with what happens in the majority of colleges as they have been with what happens in the public schools. Columbia University and Columbia Teachers College, physically separated by the width of a street, are intellectually separated by a moat as deep as ignorance. Having little in common with and little real interest in the struggles going on at the middle and lower levels, the *high* higher learning has remained aloof. It has cherished its ideals close at home, and has occasionally been scandalized by seeing such ideals abused in institutions which do not have the tradition, the students, the faculty, or the resources to uphold them.

The professional study of higher education seems certain to pass into the control of education departments of schools of second or third or tenth rank. The movement in this direction is already the cause for the kind of alarm recently expressed by the American Association of University Professors:

> The . . . Association . . . favors the strengthening of standards of graduate preparation of future college and university professors and welcomes initiative by various institutions and groups, including the regional accrediting associations, to contribute to this objective. It views with concern, however, the proposal that each state establish a professional standards board and a commission on preparation of college teachers with power to issue and revoke licenses of individual teachers at public and private institutions of higher education.[11]

The proposal referred to was made by a group known as TEPS (Teacher Education and Professional Standards) of the National Education Association. The leadership and membership in this group is chiefly "educational," chiefly from schools lacking the high professional character of the top schools. If the TEPS committee seems to be moving into an area which, in the past, was closed off to "education," it is partly because that territory has been left so blank.[12] The serious consideration of higher education, as reflected in the TEPS group and in the make-up of the last President's Conference on Higher Education, is likely to be made, not by the faculties of our greatest universities, but by laymen, professional educationists, and here and there a faculty member acting independently of his institution.

The schools of Paradise flourish as the final development of Renaissance humanism, of the quest for knowledge for the glory of man. That their intellectual efforts will end far differently from the efforts of the Scholastics who lived on the edge of Christian zeal is doubtful. The Scholastics lost God somewhere within the labyrinths of their own thought. There seems to be some danger that the modern scholars may lose man in the same misty recesses.

The heart of the matter is the unwillingness of the guardians of knowledge to examine the premises by which they live. The ruling activity and the highest value in Paradise is research. The major premise is that *all knowledge is valuable*. Except by the implications of such a curious story as that of Eve and the apple, the premise has never been seriously challenged. Academicians have stopped short, however, of making the premise *all knowledge is equally valuable*. Probably the specialist's confidence in the superiority of his own endeavors, rather than his scholarly judgment, has deterred him. Instead, he has accepted such slight modifications as *all knowledge being discovered at my university is equally valuable* and *all knowledge within my discipline or my department (or my head and card files) is more than equally valuable*.

The examination of such premises must come from on high. Any lesser voice or voices will not be heeded. A primary obligation of the schools of greatest excellence should be this task of discrimination. Part of the great energies now devoted to discovering and collecting, classifying and analyzing, could be used to examine the holdings, so to speak, to freeze some portions, to store others indefinitely, to throw some away. The university is not far different from the individual human. The past recedes and each of us stores up what we can against extinction. Some turn old bottle caps into Eiffel towers, others write official histories of family or town, others pile old magazines to the ceiling. The University should be superior to the individual, and its collective whim superior to that of any one member of it. Yet, the richer, the healthier, the more hallowed institutions become, the more they resemble family attics.

All this is not to sneer at scholarship, nor to lightly cast aside what has been so painfully assembled. It is, rather, to ask that the universities hold more by thinking larger. Our intellectual forebears need to be given rest. The inverted pyramid built upon their ghosts needs to be fashioned into a less precarious shape.

The exhaustive search to arrive at obvious conclusions needs to be stopped before it has begun. Man's brain constantly betrays him. The disinterested pursuit of truth has always been every man following his own inclination. Even if every man's inclination were guided by "right reason," the pursuit would oftentimes be misguided. When the academic man's inclination is shaped by opportunism, competition, and his own imperfections, what passes for truth may be strange indeed.

PART TWO

Within the Campus

4. The Peculiar Profession

COLLEGE teaching is, in many ways, a peculiar profession, and like many peculiar individuals, it takes a kind of pride in its peculiarities.[1] If it does not quite nurture them, it does little to inhibit their growth. Like eccentrics of many kinds, college teachers are tolerated, sometimes with fondness, more often with suspicion, by society. The cuteness of college pranks, the woolly-headedness of college professors, the irrational fervor for the old school are the clichés whereby the public hides its embarrassment over having such a peculiar old body in its midst.

Perhaps the basic oddity of the profession is the common truth that thinking is a peculiar way to earn a living. Even a college professor's children grow slowly into acceptance of thought as a meaningful occupation. Is a man sitting in a chair or staring out a window or pacing a floor doing anything? Obviously not, and he's ready to play horse, trim the hedge, hold the baby, or sign a loyalty oath without protesting that he *is* at work. The professor shares his children's suspicions. He fills his academic life less with thought than with the shuffling of papers, the meetings of committees, the going to and fro which convinces him that he is working.

In the second place, college teachers don't work regular hours. They get on the bus at 9:30 to meet a 10 o'clock class, and they may be found kicking around the garden before 5 P.M. Their comings and goings are as out of step as those of workers on a swing shift. Unlike swing shift workers, they have neither union membership nor association with goods which run and tick and go Bang!, which might win general acceptance of hours which are both irregular and flexible.

Third, the college teacher deals directly with a minority of the population, and his profession tends to be rather sharply marked off, in the mind of the public, from other occupations. Since the profession is growing and the public is becoming more familiar with it, the professor no longer seems as strange as he once did. Nevertheless, he arouses the public's suspicions about what he does and why he does it. There is really no way for a man to be in the academic profession without tipping everyone off that he is peculiar. For prospective college teachers, recognition of this truth is the beginning of wisdom.

No one has yet defined very satisfactorily what is meant by the "academic profession." The term "college teaching" would be rejected by many academicians as a proper way to describe their calling. "Teaching" is a common task which 95 per cent of academicians share, but the importance given it and the time devoted to it vary so greatly that a loose term like the "academic profession" seems to have a better fit. What this semantic confusion suggests is that a great many college teachers are not quite sure they know just what they are supposed to be doing.

College teaching, now as in the past, is split, if not fragmented by the claims of teaching, scholarship, and administration upon the teacher's time. Other professions make similar demands but with a difference. Doctors must debate general practice against specialization, and one kind of specialization against another. Lawyers have to make similar choices. So do other men in the professions. However, these choices are made during the years of preparation, and once decided upon, a medical or legal specialty furnishes a center for a future career. The prospective college teacher faces these kinds of choices, but in addition, almost throughout his career, is faced with deciding how much time he should spend on teaching, how much on research, and how much on administration. In addition, college teachers, like other professional people, are often expected to perform public services out of a sense of professional responsibility as well as from personal choice.

It may strike an outsider as odd that the teaching part of a college teacher's career is regarded with equivocation. College teachers *do* teach, and a majority find great satisfaction in the classroom. The classroom is a private domain where one can be assured of a captive audience day after day, year after year. Despite this, there exists within the profession a sense of shame about being just a teacher, and a disinclination to develop teaching into an art. It is probably the graduate schools that implant these ideas in future teachers' minds. Graduate schools emphasize scholarship and steer their students away from the quagmires of methodology to be found in teachers colleges. The Report of the President's Commission on Higher Education bluntly stated: "College teaching is the only major learned profession for which there does not exist a well-defined program of preparation directed toward developing the skills which it is essential for the practitioner to possess." [2]

This judgment is somewhat harsh. The development of a scholar, even in recondite graduate seminars like those deciphering *Finnegans Wake,* is not totally disconnected from his emergence in the classroom. Still, most college teachers do feel a shock of adjustment when their graduate work ends and their classroom duties begin, and for this the graduate schools must take the blame. Graduate schools, particularly in the humanities, prepare graduates for the kind of job which may have existed forty years ago. The job he gets today is one which calls more for an academic chameleon than for a ferret. His years of preparation lead him to expect a position at a precision grinder; instead he's put to work running errands and sweeping out the shop. Perhaps this is no one's fault. The character of higher education has changed rapidly since 1900. One generation of professors trained in one way and conditioned to one pattern of professional existence is put to work training a quite different generation of professors operating under quite different professional conditions. Institutions meet change slowly; colleges and universities exceedingly so. As a result, the beginning college teacher experiences the shock of adjusting to the teaching part of his career, and this adjustment is sometimes prolonged throughout much of his professional life.

For many college teachers, however painful the initial adjustment, actual teaching is the most pleasant part of their tasks. Done in a perfunctory manner, it is also the easiest. Perhaps it is as well that the teacher at the college level finds it difficult to confine his activities to the classroom. Teaching may be his love, but research must be his mistress.

Professors, published and unpublished, expend a good deal of energy condemning the philosophy of "publish or perish." Socrates, the argument goes, could never have held a college teaching position. The difference between Socrates and an unpublished professor aside, the necessity to publish is an academic ill that has yet to be remedied. Few of the better universities will keep faculty members who do not. Even in mediocre schools, the faculty member is rare who is not working on a monograph, a book, or continuing research which is perpetually just short of publication.

How vital much of this research and publication is, is a question the profession has never really faced. That it is vital seems to be affirmed by an increasing number of scholarly journals low on pay, long on accepted manuscripts, slow on publication, and short on readers, which provide outlets for those who in desperation or love grind it out. For the majority of the profession, the grinding takes place in the late hours and often is exceedingly fine.

If research represents an older, conservative, and basically antisocial way of meeting professional responsibilities, meeting in committees represents a newer, progressive, and highly social way. Committee meetings are one way all college teachers fulfill the third of their major duties, those of administration. At the administrative level, Parkinson's law explains the growth of academic bureaucracy. At the academic level, other forces are at work. One has only to examine the adjusted committee member to see these forces in action. There is companionship in greeting old friends at a 3:15 meeting—old friends who worked with you on the last committee or the one before that; there is opportunity in chairing a strong committee, in signing a recommendation, in rubbing shoulders with other dedicated committeemen; there is relief from care in sinking down for an afternoon to stir problems gently in the pot, savoring the aroma of full agendas, cases in point, and tabled motions. In the academic bureaucracy, administrative duties answer deep human needs.

Teaching, research, and administration: every college and university teacher must make his peace with all three. Young teachers, and not only those with eyes open to the main chance, spend much time pondering whether the slow, tedious job of scholarship is worth more than the quick response to administrative need or opportunities. Competent and incompetent teachers lament the lack of reward for good teaching. Scholars and administrators look back upon the classroom with longing. In general, the devoted teacher looks upon the intense scholar with suspicion, the scholar upon the teacher with distrust, the administrator upon both with indulgence, and all three upon the board of trustees and the legislature with faith, hope, and charity.

The conflicting demands placed upon a college teacher are a signal aspect of his profession. Such multiple responsibilities do not necessarily make the profession unattractive, though they add to the weaknesses of loose organization, widely varying professional standards and conduct, and uncertain aims which may lie behind the profession's inability to cope with recurring problems. From the individual's point of view, the diversity in professional duties may mean that an individual teacher will be allowed to develop in the direction of his strongest interest. Considering that the increasingly bureaucratic structure of the university tends toward regulation and conformity, the lack of a fixed, unified pattern of professional behavior helps to preserve a balance. Were college teaching split in this way alone, it could pride itself upon its diversity. But college teaching is pulled apart in another way, and here the status of the profession is in danger.

In many colleges and universities, college teaching has become a part-time profession.[3] College teachers, compelled by the nature of their profession to develop versatility, are further compelled by inadequate salaries to employ their versatility in ways hard to define as professional. Low salaries are still as much a touchstone of the profession as its conflicting demands. Consequently, an alarming proportion of the profession are engaged in augmenting their incomes, by professional means if possible, by hook or by crook if not.

College teachers at all ranks sell real estate, run motels, drive taxis, pick fruit, paint houses, pump gas, and perform a host of other tasks whose relation to teaching is no more obvious than these. Others earn more substantial fees at jobs more closely related to their profession: extension teaching, consultation, off-campus research, writing, and the like. The president of Louisiana State University, after making a personal study of such outside activities, observed, "Every year faculty members become more overworked, more neurotic, more weary, more irritable; their research and productive writing and teaching suffer correspondingly."[4] The three-day teaching schedule common to academic life enabled one professor to teach Monday, Wednesday, and Friday at one university and Tuesday, Thursday, and Saturday at a university nearby. By the time he was discovered, he had gained tenure at both places. Whatever they are and however they are managed, outside positions distract the college teacher from his professional duties. At worst, they make it seem that the college teacher sweating out his summers doing household chores is no professional at all.

Even were college teachers well paid, they still would find many compelling reasons for neglecting academic duties. During the past ten years, science, business, and government have bought the services of an increasing number of professors. At times, it seems that the whole world is clamoring for American experts (or Russian) to set up educational systems, sanitation projects, institutes, or to teach English or business or home economics to the world's people, or to learn about Italian art, French politics, or Indian philosophy. It is a poor professor in a shabby school who cannot find some place to go to display his expertise. However useful these activities may be, they leave many departments with a kind of floating faculty in residence, and provide one more reason for the profession's lack of a center.

The nature of college teaching contributes to the acceptance of a part-time status. The profession, recognizing the multiple responsibilities of its members, assigns comparatively few actual class hours so that the teacher will have time for preparation, correction of papers, research, and administrative duties. The public, when it is aware of the nature of a college teacher's schedule, probably misunderstands it. The absence of a time clock and with it the eight-hour day and the five-day week suggests a leisurely occupation. Add to that the frequent vacations, the whole summers off, the sabbatical leaves, why shouldn't the public look at the professor's academic duties as pleasant diversions and not deserving a full year's pay?

The world inside the university often reflects a similar point of view. The academic cliché "Publish or Perish" can be balanced by "Ph.D. and Petrify." One can complete the Ph.D., find a not very demanding position, publish a selective number of articles, take on the minimum administrative duties, work up one's steady offerings early and deviate from them never, and escape lightly from the rigors of life.

What the public knows of the academic profession is what it picks up at second or third hand. The student's firsthand experience is limited to the classroom, and the image there created is not always an impressive one. College teachers seem to lead easy lives in a pleasant atmosphere. If they are poorly paid, at least they don't have to work very hard. The parents of college students, convinced of the worth of a college education, show respect for the profession chiefly as it confers status upon their daughters and sons. The man of affairs, deferential when he needs a professor's particular knowledge or skill, is likely to find the universities a threat to free enterprise when he doesn't.

College teachers are suspicious of the polls which show them enjoying a status just short of that of the top half dozen professions.[5] The poll takers may be right. A professor is one of those persons who should be respected, and people who answer polls often respond in ways they feel they *should*, rather than with feelings which will later motivate their actions. The flooding of our colleges with all manner of applicants suggests that higher education enjoys public respect in considerable measure. On the other hand, the level of public support suggests that such respect does not affect the public very deeply. The abuses still perpetrated upon college faculties by legislatures, presidents, boards of trustees, alumni, and the general public testify to a status which is at best equivocal. The antagonism between town and gown in communities which rub shoulders with academicians is not mere proof that familiarity breeds contempt. Status is a lure which the profession possesses principally because the illusion of status is often present in the minds of the kinds of persons who are likely to become college professors.

College teaching does have its attractive aspects, and for the bright young man who has fallen in love with college life, it is a way of prolonging the affair. As with other campus romances, the passion and the glory wear off as the lover's embrace becomes a domestic entanglement. This romantic illusion, seldom dispelled before the affected is head-deep in a doctoral dissertation and knee-deep in children, explains why a good many men get into academic life as a result of drift rather than self-direction. The profession is not hostile to such men; it often protects them, coddles them, and seldom tries to break the spell.

For other individuals, the challenge of college teaching, the hard work it entails, is its strongest attraction. The classroom load and the schedule are inaccurate measures of the energy expended in college teaching. The time spent in the classroom is usually three to five hours per day three days a week, or the equivalent. The vacant hours are filled with students and meetings, with the marking of papers and assigning of grades, and with preparing for the next day's or next hour's lectures. Doing all these conscientiously fills an eight-hour day though not necessarily the scholar's mind. The kind of continuing reading and writing and experimenting a man must do if he is to profess honestly takes place outside the usual working hours. In this as in other professions, such conditions are not regarded as drawbacks to a career; rather they mark the intense involvement with one's chosen work which draws a man to a profession and which satisfies his most deeply felt ambitions.

Like other professions, college teaching has a way of becoming a life. For a conscientious teacher, breaking away from the job is almost impossible. When a professor does shake himself away from his books, though not often from his colleagues and their shop talk, his social life is probably not as appalling as it has been described by some modern novelists. Social life varies widely from one level of college to another. In all of them, it is probably centered around the profession, but in this respect it probably does not differ from doctors entertaining other doctors, lawyers other lawyers and the like. Since college teaching is characterized by diversity within its system of departments and disciplines, social life, though inseparable from professional life, may be more varied and interesting than that found among other professional groups.

College teaching is a clean profession. The dirt and grime tend to disappear among the ivy. Even political and social crises have a way of getting resolved, albeit superficially, by historical perspective and scholarly detachment. Moderation, deliberation, and judicial calm have their depressing aspects, and some faculty members probably find academic serenity both vexing and sinful. Life on a college faculty may be threatened by dullness and isolation, but in a world where privacy is both necessary and difficult to attain, the detachment of college life is likely to attract more young people than it repels.

Within the calm of academic life, there are enough individuals of differing temperaments and persuasions to create a continual mild stir. The individuality of college faculty members is the glory and despair of any director of an academic group. Individualism exists within limits—real subversives are few as are hardened criminals—but as yet no single bolt of gray flannel would clothe an entire college faculty. At the same time, the individuality which arises from specialization offers a diversity of knowledge and outlooks which the academic community can share. The chance to preserve one's individuality and to respond to the individuality of others, even within an enclosed milieu, is not to be dismissed lightly.

Finally, the college teacher, apart from his subject matter, deals directly with developing human beings, not with their organs, their aberrations, or their mass behavior, but with the whole being. The contact made is living and yet abstract, leaving the teacher free but always a part of the developing lives around him. It deals with human beings at their richest point: with girls who bounce instead of sag, with boys between the cloddishness of fifteen and the bullishness of twenty-five. Here, surely, is the main appeal that college teaching can offer.

The question for the professor and his profession in the decade ahead is whether the appeal of college teaching will be strong enough to attract the required number of bright young men and women. The estimates of new teachers needed by 1970 vary from 180,000 to 480,000; the estimates of doctorates likely to be produced from 120,000 to 160,000.[6] About 60 per cent of these are likely to go into higher education. Whatever estimates prove correct, and counting all who might be lured into the profession, it is going to be very difficult to staff college faculties adequately in the years ahead.

There is some basis for hope that colleges will continue to attract men and women of high intellect. In the competition for brains and talent, higher education, despite its salaries, has done well. It has a great attraction for bright young men and women from the middle class or below. The opportunities for higher education are independent of family and social position in a way that opportunities in business often are not. The capital investment can be spread out, and the chance of financial aid is always good for those of exceptional ability. For young people brought up in modest circumstances, the full life in pleasant surroundings has special value, as does the kind of prestige they associate with college and college professors. On the other hand, the world outside the university is likely to become increasingly attractive in comparison with the university itself. Small colleges are impoverished as never before. Large schools have become huge, and even a lover of alma mater and the life of the mind can transfer both affections to large corporations without great loss. The complete life is being subsidized by private industry in a way that only college life afforded in the past. It is often difficult to tell whether one is driving by a new industrial plant or a new college campus, and the necessaries of intellectual endeavor are generously provided those willing to leave the campus for the corporation. In short, the world and the college have come much closer together, and the college has lost part of its traditional appeal.

At close range, it may seem possible that such a peculiar profession as college teaching will find the large numbers of competent men and women it needs. When one steps back and surveys the American college campus from a higher vantage point, perceiving its inflated athleticism, its continual begging for existence, its flexible goals and standards, its confusion of purpose, its fostering of mass behavior and exclusiveness, its history of compromise and defensive action, its willingness to be led rather than to lead—the possibility does not seem very strong.

The shortage of college teachers in the next decade is likely to be met as other vital academic problems have been met in the past: by expedients which turn into policy and tradition. Having a body of teachers too few in number and spotty in quality will tend to accent the profession's existing weaknesses. The teacher's multiple duties will probably become more pressing and less satisfying. Salaries may rise, but so will class loads, paper work, and administrative duties. A profession, hard pressed to attract teachers now, will become more hard pressed still. No one need fear that higher education will collapse for want of professors. Football stadiums will be bigger, parking lots more vast, administrative structures more complex. For among the profession's characteristics, call it a peculiarity if you will, is the ability to live with its problems without either bringing them to a solution or collapsing under their weight.

5. "Student Life"

IDEALLY, college professors are the tutors of civilization. Not only do they help savage youth become civilized man, but they help civilization itself move further away from savagery. As older and wiser beings whose passion is truth, professors pass on to students the grave responsibility of preserving enlightenment in various times of darkness and of adding to the sum of the world's knowledge and culture. These are the noble sentiments which the colleges profess; what happens on the campus day by day reveals how easily high thoughts become lowly platitudes. Professors are not quite baby sitters, nor do they yet fix their students' cars, but they teach *matrology* (that's motherhood) and *patrology* (that's fatherhood), and they make up college catalogues more packed with wonders than a seed catalogue. It is ironic that American mothers and fathers periodically fear that their children in college will fall under the influence of alien ideas and radical professors. If a student took many of the classes in most of the nation's universities, he would run into ideas that are alien chiefly to the development of the mind. If he fell completely under the spell of a wily professor, he would learn truckling, evasion, and compromise, part of the Life Education curriculum and as orthodox as basketball.

The classics, the humanities, the unsocial sciences still occupy their niches in many colleges and universities. A handful have high standards of admission. There are some colleges in which more students are taking second-year French than ninth-grade arithmetic. But within the majority of American institutions of higher education, the student body [1] has long ago diagnosed the faculty as a nagging but not fatal pain, a chronic ache which flares up only during examination weeks. When the pain becomes too intense, counselors, advisers, and student-welfare committees are available to prescribe remedies. Despite the clinical efficiency of these groups and individuals, student conduct is not much better today than it was in those days before college athletics were invented to make institutional capital out of masculine energies.[2] One thing *is* certain. Student life is better organized.

There are few American campuses where the student union and the administration building are not the most impressive structures—the stadium excepted, of course. Here and there, a library may run a poor third. The student union symbolizes the full life which almost all American colleges and universities now provide for their students. Only a curmudgeon would question its role in the total educational experience. The question is not whether bowling has a vital role in higher education but whether the alleys should be air-conditioned. To make certain, perhaps, that the students' investment in the Union Building is sound, the administrations have invested at least as much in men, office space, and equipment to see that students "live." [3] No other word can cover the multitude of activities over which the Office of Student Affairs or the Student Life Committee or whatever it is called has jurisdiction.

A Student Union Building is easier to build than a classroom building, for student fees can be used to meet the mortgage payments on the Union. Once built, the Union has to have someone to run it. A new campus organization, complete with Director, Assistant Directors, Secretaries, and Managers of everything from Purchasing to Ping-Pong, comes into existence. Such large numbers of persons, augmented by a swarm of students looking for Activity Credits, make certain that few hours of the day or night are left open for classroom activities, library work, or contemplation.

Quite apart from the busy offices of those who run social life at the Union are the offices of the Dean of Students. In larger institutions, the offices of the Dean of Men and the Dean of Women are now but two wings of this much larger structure. Each major office has its assistants, its branch managers, its secretarial staff. The Director of the Counseling Service, of Student Behavior, of Foreign Student Affairs (a recent addition), of Marriage and Family Counseling, of Placement, of Panhellenic Activities, of the Dormitory System—all of these add up to an administrative group which is second only to the President's office in size and complexity. Combined with the Union staff, it is probably larger.

What do all these people do (for convenience, I use the term "Student Affairs" to refer to them and their activities), and what does their presence mean to campus life? Universities are large communities, and though they exist within other communities, they necessarily assume the services which citizens expect of any community: police and fire protection, street maintenance, garbage collection, recreation, public health, and welfare. These services in a university community, however, are not the concern of Student Affairs. They belong to Building and Grounds or to Maintenance or to some other separate entity. These divisions differ from the Office of Student Affairs in a number of ways. First, they do not directly and constantly meddle in academic matters. Second, most of the services they perform are necessary. Third, they perform services which the citizens of an ordinary community cannot or do not choose to do for themselves. The Office of Student Affairs not only takes on a host of responsibilities best left to the citizen, but seems to assume that the citizens are not only indigent but brainless as well.

A long time ago, the Dean of Men and the Dean of Women were chiefly responsible for seeing that the outside life of the students did not interfere grossly with their academic pursuits. They were also responsible for disciplining students and groups whose actions were harmful to the college community. Both duties were pushed aside long ago. The modern Office of Student Affairs is dedicated to everything that interferes with academic life. Such offices are mainly occupied in organizing the pernicious pleasures they have helped bring into existence. The best way to illuminate their activities is to chart the growth of a typical campus passion.

The Song Fest will serve as well as any. Its history is not a part of academic history, though, considering its present impact upon the student's education, it should be. For some reason, some students love to sing in groups. College songs have a history as old as the colleges. Perhaps the good fellowship one finds on campus produces a natural desire to harmonize about it. On the face of it, group singing is a harmless enough activity.

Its gradual development into a campus-wide competitive sport may have begun with a beery remark that our boys can sing better than your boys, or a less truculent challenge from one sorority to another. However it developed, such close harmony was certain to be picked up by someone on the staff of the Office of Student Affairs. The possibilities must have been immediately recognized. Why not formalize these rich outpourings of college sentiment? Why not make them a tradition? Why not bring in the dormitory boys and girls and make the higher harmony complete? Why not make it the spring counterpart of football?

The results can be heard on any campus any spring. Like football, group singing, pushed along by professional games-makers, became intensely competitive. Practice sessions became longer. Ringers were brought in from outlying choirs. A diversion became an obsession. The competition moved from the social rooms to the auditorium and finally to the stadium and fieldhouse. Everyone was singing. Everyone was happy. Except perhaps a handful of surly professors who wondered why spring quarter work sank even more abysmally than unorganized love and lust could account for.

When the faculty bothered to complain, the Student Affairs Officers responded as professionally as before. They drew up regulations. They restricted practice hours. They composed a code of ethical conduct, defined proper recruiting practices, and limited subsidization. To satisfy the pedants, the whole event, practice sessions and all, was to take place outside of class hours. Students, now forced to practice at 5 A.M. or 10 P.M., chalked up one more mark against the professors. They ate breakfast during their eight o'clocks and slept through the rest. A half-quarter went by in painful anticipation of Song Fest night. After that, the rest of the quarter was anticlimax, as schoolwork had been all quarter long.

This sketch neglects the positive merits of singing competitively. Song Fests, say the Activities Chairmen, are better than Spring Riots, better than Panty Raids, better than illicit sexual activity under the elms. From the Student Affairs point of view, perhaps so. Certainly for the students, Song Fest is less exciting, less a release of emotions and energies, less fun, and probably less educational. For the faculty, a riot is over in a night; Song Fest goes on for weeks; and there is no end at all to the formalized fun which Student Affairs experts think up to channel the students' libidinal energies into socially acceptable and growth-promoting and citizenship-enhancing and group-developing activities.

The prevailing philosophy of the Office of Student Affairs is an intense activism. Part of this fervor, particularly in democratic state universities, is a kind of perverse response to the undemocratic practices of sororities and fraternities. It is passé to write passionately of the evils of fraternity and sorority life, passé because the Student Affairs offices have tried to make life among the barbarians as much like fraternity and sorority life as possible. The unaffiliated have gained the social graces at the price of losing control over most of their social life. Only the size of the dormitory systems makes it possible for a student with a mildly academic turn of mind to work quietly and alone. Were it not that big dormitory units can be constructed more cheaply than smaller ones, even that possibility would disappear. And already the Offices of Student Affairs have established their branches in the dormitories, sent out their social workers to see that no drudge in a back room tries to violate the spirit of the good life.

The fraternities and sororities and the values they espouse give greatest scope for the ambitions of the Offices of Student Affairs. A fat, prosperous America where every plebeian boy or girl can go to college finds social distinctions more important than ever. Administrators smile upon fraternity and sorority houses as adjuncts to the dormitory system. Here and there, democratic practices are pumped into the system to nationwide publicity. Despite the current favor it is enjoying, the fraternity and sorority system remains opposed not only to an individual's right of privacy but to democracy and to scholarship. This means that a large part of the Student Affairs energies are devoted to putting the system in a good light.

At most universities, to single out one aspect, rushing is as strictly regulated as athletic scholarships. When a faculty protests against the time rushing takes from the school year, the Student Affairs group is happy to make adjustments. Putting rush activities completely outside the academic year would work a hardship on rushees and houses, so a compromise is made. "Pre-rush" is inaugurated. It takes up approximately twice as much time outside the school year but only half as much inside, at least at the beginning. In a short time, its dimensions will expand and the academic year will be blighted by both "prerush" and "rush" activities. Still, the Student Affairs group has done its best to maintain academic standards.

Such dry-cleaning requires a great amount of staff time. It is not directly faculty time, of course. The faculty absently approves the latest plan brought to the Faculty Senate by the Student Affairs Panhellenic Chairman. Fraternity and sorority life are part of the curriculum, and no one tampers with someone else's class offerings.

A final example of activities strongly urged by Student Affairs is the spawning and nurturing of student governments. As the handmaidens of democracy, Student Affairs officers take pride in giving the student real experience in the democratic process. Fine as this is in theory, in practice, student government becomes a "fun" activity indistinguishable from planning the Junior Prom. Nevertheless, campuses vibrate to the noise of campaigns; large numbers of students paint posters, make speeches, and register a handful of voters at the polls. Some get elected. Student Senates meet and pass resolutions, even legislation. Student Courts settle cases. National groups entice delegates to national conventions. And for what? Certainly for no remarkable increase either in responsible citizenship or in political intelligence if we can judge from the behavior of college students after graduation.[4] The more obvious results are the many hours lost to disciplining the mind, to finding a vocation, to preparing one's skills, and to increasing one's knowledge for some kind of life that demands more than an ability to play games.

Student government, to be worth the energy expended on it, should be more than a benevolently sustained illusion of democracy on campus. The Student Affairs office, largely responsible for this illusion, finds itself in a curious position. On the one hand, it helps the students draw up constitutions, run their elections, and execute their decisions. On the other, it has to be constantly on guard that the student government's actions never infringe upon the touchy areas where the administration (and less often the faculty) has jurisdiction. Consequently, it spends its time elaborating a fiction rather than attempting to increase the students' awareness of political reality.

Like many other activities on college campuses which are adverse to education, "student affairs" are tolerated by a majority of the faculty. Or rather, the faculty, seeing them firmly entrenched as a part of the academic enterprise, feels neither the right nor the responsibility to question their existence.

Occasionally, the faculty is drawn into making an uncomfortable choice. Student publications serve a more real need than student governments, if only because their activities have to be thought out sufficiently to be written down. Student newspapers are inane enough, but where there is a spark of undergraduate imagination, sometimes even intellect, it often shows itself here. To the Office of Student Affairs, such sparks are dangerous. When they get scattered abroad by publication in the student paper, they are horrifying.

Many universities have felt the sting of criticism from the student paper. At my own university not long ago, the student paper published a puerile letter reflecting adversely on the prevailing church. The events which followed were both humiliating and characteristic. The Office of Student Affairs, responding to the anger of the administration, called the students to account. The students stood upon their right of freedom of the press. The Publications Council, a joint faculty-student committee directly responsible for publications, became the agents for a mild but not very subtle suppression. In the minds of many students, members of the faculty were advocates of tyranny and betrayers of the truths they preached. Given one show of unorthodoxy in a paper which might have been suppressed long before for asininity, the faculty seemed ready to abjure their most sacred vows.

Student magazines cause a similar kind of trouble.[5] Again, I draw upon experience, not because it is unusual, but because it is typical. For the past year, I have served on the Publications Council. As a result of the newspaper incident just mentioned, a special faculty adviser to student publications was appointed. He was not a censor—of course—merely a giver of good advice which the students—of course—would always accept. Our adviser was astute enough in newspaper matters, but rather blunt in literary ones. No one can win the confidence of editors of campus literary magazines, anyway. They are, in the manner of literary youth, dedicated to getting life as they see it into the pages of their magazine. A literary magazine's span of untroubled existence is that period between an editor's appointment and the appearance of S-E-X in its pages. The period is always short.

One morning, my phone rang. The publications adviser was on the line. Once we had exchanged pleasantries, he went directly to the point. "It's a poem," he said. "It's got a whore in it." The poem certainly did, and the student editor wanted to print it, and, in addition, a story with "hell," "Lord," and one or two saltier expletives. For days, the joint committee tried to resolve an impossible dilemma. The students, resting their case on the principles of freedom of the press, on the lessons their faculty members had taught them, on the examples of modern literature on every newsstand, and on the fiction of total responsibility given to the Associated Students of the University, wanted the right to print what they would. The faculty, swearing to protect the students' rights, wanting to give full scope to their creative efforts, and refusing to become censors, did not want—could not have—a poem with a whore in it. Eventually, through a strained but acceptable compromise, the poem was withheld. The relative lubricity of each of the offending words in the story was arrived at mathematically, and a trade was worked out between a half-dozen words of one kind and two or three of another. The citizens' committee which had called upon the president to protest a previous story in the magazine was spared a second trip. The magazine continues to be published. The same thing is certain to happen again. Among many feckless campus activities, student publications could be of real value in developing campus intellectual life. But the administration, the Office of Student Affairs, and many of the faculty, have been most happy when what the students print has been as vapid as can only be expected of undergraduates under benevolent faculty advisement.

The criticisms of extracurricular activities will do nothing to change the character of campus life. The universities have sanctioned the creation of a professional group whose duty is creating, perpetuating, and administering such activities. The genius of the American university, as contrasted with that of other institutions, is its capacity to create positions within itself for all those it has trained to be useless elsewhere. The campus is a pleasant place. It was a pleasant place long before its pleasures were worked into the catalogue. The presence of a plague of extracurricular activities of spontaneous growth would be a good deal better than the perpetual good health campaigns carried on by doctors of fellowship and nurses of compatibility.

What gives point to this complaint is that the students themselves don't seem greatly attracted to organized student life. "Interest in student groups, clubs, even fraternities," the ACE Commission on the College Student observed in 1958, "has steadily dwindled, except perhaps for the freshman who is trying to find his footing in the new world of college life. . . . Organized activities seem 'collegiate'—and this is no longer a word of praise." The Commission's report goes on:

Even on campuses where there is an elaborate system of student organizations and activities, studies suggest that only about one-third of the student body participates in it to any extent. For example, in one study consulted, it is evident that the activity program was of greatest interest to those students who were already participating in their fraternity and sorority activities, so that the campus program served only to provide an extended range of activity for this already active minority.[6]

In light of these observations, it is significant that in Knapp's and Greenbaum's study of the collegiate origins of younger American scholars, the first twelve institutions are ones in which "the social fraternity system is either extremely weak, inactive, or nonexistent." [7]

The worst part of all this is that university faculties have created student "life." Despite the powers which faculties could have to impose guild requirements, they have let every handicrafter set up a stall. Student Affairs offices are not staffed by nonacademic personnel. They are under the control of full professors and associate professors and assistant professors and instructors with fresh Ph.D.'s in Table Setting and Group Dynamics. Where were the righteous academicians when Ph.D. programs were approved in the Department of Health, Recreation, and Physical Education? Where were they when the final examinations were being given? Where were they when Family Living became a course, then a department, and finally a College? At the Song Fest, probably, or at the Stadium, or serving hot dogs to the new freshmen.

6. The Playing Fields

To right-thinking men everywhere, college football is and has been from its inception a beastly sport. Its players are snake-hipped and ox-headed; its coaches have the guile of foxes and the hides of elephants; its supporters roar like the lion and bray like the ass. Yet the beast survives. Over almost every college campus its banner flies: head in helmet, heart on a chalk-striped field, hand outstretched.

The alchemy which unites pigskin and egghead is as mysterious as the reasons why college presidents become positive boobies when they contemplate the glories of their athletic programs. Every year, college professors damn big-time athletics. Every two or three years, a committee meets to investigate. Every decade, writers summarize athletics' sorry record. Seldom has so thoroughly discredited an activity maintained such vigorous life and in such high-principled company.

What is new, if anything, about this old sordid story is that college athletics today have won full acceptance as legitimate university activities, and with acceptance, tacit approval of practices which even a backward school might have frowned upon twenty-five years ago. College athletics thrive today chiefly because of corrupt practices which have been incorporated into codes of legitimate conduct.

Initially, intercollegiate athletics gained a place in the universities, insofar as academic men had anything to do with it, as a result of idealism, wistfulness, and expediency. *Mens sana in corpore sano* was the classical ideal which obscured the dubious relationship. At the same time, the wistfulness which men who spend their lives chasing abstractions often feel toward violent physical contact lent attractiveness to the ideal. For university presidents facing the necessity of distilling raw animal spirits into purer forms, football seemed a likely expedient. That it could add to a college's fame and increase its income made its expediency certain.

Once established, college athletics drew heavily upon ambition, pride, and sentimentality. In the Midwest, where football frenzy was passed on from the East, personal sentiments were mixed with the universities' ambitions and the states' pride. Schools without traditions manufactured them. In Iowa, a pig became one of the spoils of victory. He was called Floyd of Rosedale and was probably the only personality in the state who didn't much care whether Iowa beat Minnesota. All over the land, the newspapers ground out stories about heart and grit and playing the game.

Today, these simpler impulses of the past have been largely replaced by the philosophy of mercenary idealism: the outstretched hand and the question, "How much?" An army of recruiters sells the full free ride like pardoners peddling indulgences. An eternity of losing seasons yawns for the coach who fails to exact his tithes. "At Iowa State," said the young coach who was leaving for Texas A. & M., "I had very little money to develop my athletic dreams. There was little money in the budget, little money for recruiting athletes and not much in the way of facilities to attract the athletes we could contact. There is no comparison between our facilities now at College Station and at Iowa State. For example, we have seven new cars assigned to the athletic department, and I can't wait to get home to see our new athletic dormitory. We have spaces for 92 student-athletes in this new building and the entire building is air-conditioned and we have wall-to-wall carpeting." [1]

Recruiting is at the center of the corruption which marks big-time college sports. In 1929, the Carnegie investigation called subsidizing and recruiting "the most disgraceful phase" of intercollegiate athletics. Today, recruiting flourishes, sanctioned by a code which is not so much a guide to conduct as a measure of earning power. Under the NCAA regulations, when financial aid to an athlete "exceeds commonly accepted educational expenses (tuition and fees, room and board, books, and not to exceed $15 per month for laundry) . . . it shall be considered to be 'pay' for participation." The principles regulating recruiting activities are equally delicate. Coaches cannot offer more than the free ride; each college gets to pay for the prospect's visit to the campus one time "and one time only"; the prospect cannot bring along relatives or girl-friends except at his own expense; entertainments are restricted to two days and two nights and must not be "excessive." It is as if banks condoned embezzlement as long as the embezzlers followed the regulations set forth by the National Board of Peculation.

How far athletics have developed in thirty years can be roughly measured by comparing present legitimate practices with the practices criticized in the Carnegie Foundation report. Henry S. Pritchett, summarizing the findings, wrote:

> The paid coach, the special training tables, the costly sweaters and extensive journeys in special Pullman cars, the recruiting from the high school, the demoralizing publicity showered on the players, the devotion of an undue proportion of time to training, the devices for

putting a desirable athlete, but a weak scholar, across the hurdles of the examinations—these ought to stop and the intercollege and intramural sports be brought back to a stage in which they can be enjoyed by a large number of students and where they do not involve an expenditure of time and money wholly at variance with any ideal of honest study.[2]

None of these practices have stopped. The NCAA, which shared the feeling for reform in the 1920's, has brought most of these activities in under the code. That those involved in athletics still find ways to violate the rules proves that intercollegiate athletics does, indeed, sharpen the wits. The recurring scandals—basketball fixing, cheating, tampering with academic records, condoned brutality, contract-jumping, slush funds—suggest that weakening the code has not strengthened the character.

For the athletic mess, the universities have themselves to blame. The NCAA, though top-heavy in its administration with coaches and athletic directors, is a college and university body. As long ago as 1922, it adopted a resolution urging "absolute faculty control" of athletics. And though faculty members of football universities know how far from "absolute" even absolute faculty control is, they probably have more control than they have ever exercised. The reasons they haven't are not hard to find.

In the first place, American colleges and universities have never been much concerned with the intellectual life. The full life and the free ride are quite compatible philosophies. The colleges and universities that do honor the intellectual life are those like Reed, Antioch, Chicago, Johns Hopkins, which do not maintain big-time athletics, or those, like the Ivy League schools which have achieved in recent years a measure of deemphasis. It is well to remember that the level of intellectual life in the Ivy League schools when football grew to power was probably not much higher than it is in the state universities today.

In the state universities, now the chief supporters of inflated athletic programs, the intellectual life is the concern of a small group at best. The liberal arts college within the state university is often the most keen in its criticism of the university's athletic practices, but even within this college, faculty members hold widely differing views. Some genuinely enjoy the game. Others tolerate it as one among many human follies. Many are creatures of habit, and being in the stadium on Saturday afternoons is not much different from being in the supermarket on Saturday mornings.

When Phi Beta Kappa refused to grant new chapters to institutions whose aid to athletes was out of proportion to aid granted other students, faculty members from some liberal arts colleges objected to such a firm stand. They pointed out, with some justice, that the regulations were not being applied to existing Phi Beta Kappa chapters. With less justice and a shrinking sense of responsibility, they argued that the liberal arts college was too small to control university policy and that the liberal arts college breathed a purer air than that of the fieldhouse. Phi Beta Kappa has stood by its principles, but it is virtually the only organization within or related to the academic cosmos that has.

In the second place, college and university faculties are singularly inept at doing anything about their problems. Academic protests against low salaries have been as numerous, and as futile, as those against athletics. Members of faculty senates, fierce exponents of democracy, inveigh against the fraternity and sorority system and then approve the appointment of one more assistant dean of student life to assist in interfraternity affairs. Cheating in the classroom, autocracy in the administration building, and an entangling bureaucracy throughout the campus are other problems which were long ago placed on the committee agenda and which have never been taken off.

Third, the athletic departments have flummoxed the academicians by playing their kind of game. They have become research departments, amassing books and monographs, acquiring equipment, and graduating M.A.'s and Ph.D.'s. An academic department of any kind is as hard to dislodge as an ape from a tree. When it has stored up the fruits of research, it is invulnerable. On the playing field, coaches operate within a complex of scouts, spies, and spotters equipped with binoculars, field phones, and wrist radios. Off the field, they read monographs like "Two and Three Dimensional Slide Images Used with Tachistoscopic Training Techniques in Instructing Football Players in Defenses," or articles beginning, "Bat selection is a profoundly important task." [3] Such absurdities of title and profundities of thought are, of course, not uncommon to other academic periodicals, but no other journals are so solemn and so pious. Only in *The Athletic Journal,* "America's First Coaching Magazine," is one likely to find the "Huddle Prayer," specially written for the Pop Warner Conference for Kiddie Football by Father Cavanagh of Notre Dame, Rabbi Max Klein, and Norman Vincent Peale:

> Grant us the strength, Dear Lord, to play
>   This game with all our might;
> And while we're doing it we pray
>   You'll keep us in your sight;
> That we may never say or do
>   A thing that gives offense to you.

Finally, the vast momentum the game has picked up over the years rolls over the most strenuous efforts at reform. Today's players become the boosters and the coaches for the next generation, and in many states, the high school principals and superintendents. College publicity departments grind out the copy upon which the daily newspapers feed. To the sports fraternity, as they call themselves, the existence of big-time athletics in the universities is proof enough that they are desirable and relevant activities. "While there will be a segment of the egg-head species in educational circles," a sports editor wrote recently, "that abhors even the hint of physical exertion aside from the pursuit and capture of academic degrees, the average professor looks upon athletic activity in a true light." [4]

There is some evidence that athletic handouts are beginning to cause indigestion. Bud Wilkinson warned his fellow coaches in 1959 that students weren't going out for football.[5] "Part of it," he said, "is probably due to the fact that we all contact athletes. If a boy doesn't get a scholarship then he apparently feels unwanted." Ten years ago at Oklahoma, the freshman squad consisted of 110 athletes. In 1959, only 37 turned out, 27 of whom were on athletic scholarships. The glory of varsity sports, always a dubious reward for the hamburger squads, is today pretty much proportional to the cash received, and the price of hamburger is going up. The cost of athletic programs is as hard to find out as an office-mate's salary, but certainly the majority of big athletic programs lose money, some a great deal of money. The Big Ten schools spend an average of over $150,000 a year in aid to athletes.[6] In 1937–1938, some Big Ten schools were spending less on total athletic assistance than they now spend bringing prospective athletes to the campus as a part of legitimate recruiting. Partly because of the expense, the number of colleges playing football dropped from 709 in 1940, to 690 in 1947, and to 623 in 1959. Last year, both Marquette University and the University of Denver gave up football. As costs increase, even more will give up the sport.

The recruiting of players has had another consequence. In football, players are bought by the pound; in basketball, by the yard. High school athletes of ordinary dimensions, however impressive their records, are not prime prospects for athletic scholarships. The catering to exceptional physical specimens has separated college athletics from the spectators and from the undergraduates whose duty it is to whip up frenzy for the game. Gigantism, specialization of function, and intensive coaching have not made the team sports better spectacles. Despite tinkering with the rules, basketball threatens to score itself out of public interest and football to expire from interminable delays.

The changing character of higher education also seems to be having an impact upon big-time athletics. Columbia's president was reported in my local paper as telling his alumni, "I hope you may feel that some of the prestige Columbia has lost in football in these years has been offset by the award of four Nobel Prizes to Columbia men in the last three years and of another Nobel Prize this year to another Columbia College graduate." The chancellor of the University of Denver, Chester Alter, flatly predicted that the days of big-time football were numbered. California, a West Coast reporter wrote, is going Ivy League. And James Morrill, president emeritus of Minnesota, defended a losing coach: "Athletic entertainment is not the primary purpose of the University of Minnesota or the justification for its existence."[7]

This last remark from the Midwest, a region passionately attached to football, basketball, and funny papers, is a significant one. There is logic in thinking that the Big Ten schools may before long deemphasize, and there are some signs.[8] The Ohio State alumni magazine has been conducting a continuing campaign against overemphasis; faculties of other conference schools have been making their objections felt. The split vote over continuing the Rose Bowl contract involved many of the schools in a curious moral dilemma. Minnesota forfeited its chance even for a moral victory in accepting the 1961 Rose Bowl invitation—and lost 17-7—despite its having voted against participation. The faculty senate at Ohio State, which had also voted against continuing the contract, voted 21 to 20 to accept its share of the receipts. Minnesota, Ohio State, Wisconsin, Michigan, and others have the physical facilities, the faculties, and can select the students that would make them primarily intellectual institutions. States are already seeing the wisdom and the economy of using the smaller public and private colleges as the general undergraduate college and of reserving the state university for a *higher* higher education. The subordination of sports to intellect in the Big Ten would do much to restore sanity to college athletics.

Even now, there is some comfort in thinking that big-time sports are maintaining themselves largely on the accumulated glories of the past. This would explain why, on college faculties, the support for football comes from aging professors of the classics as well as from young professors of athletic administration. Those faculty members nearing retirement age now were undergraduates in the golden days of the sport. They had Knute Rockne in the flesh. The young professors had to settle for Pat O'Brien. Those now in the graduate school lack even that.

If athletics do subside, it will not be because of moral indignation, and its decline will be attended by wailing and weeping and gnashing of teeth. Recognition of a changing attitude toward sports, if such an attitude comes about, will come slowly to the booster clubs, the athletic departments, and the newspapers. These groups have never been disturbed by the disparity between the shoddiness of athleticism and the high purposes of a university. They have preserved the myths of sport long after such myths have lost what small part of truth they may have once possessed.

The melancholy truth is that reached by Plato long ago. Man's glory is his reason, but it exists at the small end of the triangle. He carries with him "the heavy bear," and in the end as in the beginning the beast will have him. Civilization is still a clearing in the jungle, and if apes gambol in the public square no one should be surprised. That they should have gained such a high place in the halls of learning is as flattering to the beasts as it is humiliating to man.

7. The Bureaucracy

THE war between college faculties and administrations is one of higher education's longest inconclusive struggles. The administrative command is today comfortably established behind rank upon rank of secretarial and service personnel and covered at every exposed position by an IBM 702. Against this force, the faculty has only the harassing fire of peevish complaint. If the faculty were not so intent on containing the administration, and the administration so intent on subduing the faculty, both might recognize that their common enemy is a mindless bureaucracy which stalks both camps. It could hardly be otherwise. Bring together a large number of students reluctant to learn, a faculty reluctant to teach, an administration reluctant to administer, and a public reluctant to let any of these activities go on without suspecting treason, and bureaucracy is the result. For only a bureaucracy can render learning harmless and yet preserve the appearance of accomplishment.

Despite the great numbers coming into college, American students come reluctantly to learning. They come because of family obligations or the desire for prestige or because they've been encouraged to put off work and to demean all occupations which do not require a college degree.[1] A small number have the kind of intense desire which, in the Middle Ages, sought out professors and formed the guilds which became European universities. At Bologna in the thirteenth century, students controlled the university and fined their professors for being late to class, for getting behind in the text, or for failing to attract at least five students to a lecture.[2] That kind of zeal passed away long ago, as did direct student control of the universities. Unresponsive as the students often are, the American university has always been keenly responsive to their desires. The classical curriculum of the nineteenth century passed away not only because of a change in educational philosophy, but because it failed to attract the students. The rise of graduate education was not alone a response to expanding knowledge, but a response to the students' leaving America for education in Europe. Higher education today is standardized, formalized, and quantified because the students have arrived at one end of the process and means must be found to get them to the other.

The average university begins by assuming that the students have had no previous education, no previous physical exercise, and no experience with human beings beyond their immediate families. After their bodiless selves have been run through the processing machines, they face a first year routine as demeaning as this:

First Semester	Second Semester
Orientation	Adjustment to Business
Freshman Composition	Speech
Physical Education I	Bowling
Health Education I	Courtship and Marriage
Living in Society	Understanding Sculpture
Chemistry	Military Science [3]

All of these large general courses require section heads, section hands, area supervisors, program coordinators, departmental advisers, general counselors, and clerks to record the transactions. By the employment of many human beings, the universities convince themselves that the mechanics of education has not overwhelmed its personal character.

For this, the students are not precisely responsible, though their dependence upon the system does much to keep it strong. Certainly there is a correlation between the students' dependence and the vagueness and torpor of their educational aspirations. Having no clear idea of where they are going, they let the college provide both direction and impetus. The colleges have provided courses for every conceivable vocational objective and tailored the courses to suit the weakest students' faint enthusiasms.

Above all, the colleges have embraced the granting of credits and the assigning of grades as the means of giving students, parents, and faculty immediate and continuing assurance that they are not engaged in a fruitless enterprise. The students may learn little, but they quickly develop faith in the credit system, the simple transaction upon which the bureaucracy depends. When students are animated most, it is not by the content of the course but by the prospect of getting five hours of A. Seniors never write so well as when they request waivers of credit in order to graduate.

The credit system is one of the large academic sins. Upon it depends the dull student whose A's in tether-ball and leadership offset E's in reading and numbers. So does the honor student whose total grade point average may mean election to Phi Beta Kappa or to Phi Kappa Phi or to the ultimate honorary which will include the upper 95 per cent. So does the professor, and so does the administration, and for that matter, so does the public. As it exists now, the credit system is unassailable. No one planned it; no one nurtured it; no one is responsible for it; but everyone is dependent upon it. Having supported generations of bookkeepers when the universities were concerned with books, it now supports families of machines at a time when the universities are concerned with machines.

A scholarly investigation of the growth of the credit system appeared in the *AAUP Bulletin* (Winter, 1955).[4] The writer, Dietrich Gerhard, traced its beginnings to public demands for a more varied list of courses and more practical courses in both high schools and colleges in the 1870's and 1880's. The most influential individual was Charles W. Eliot, president of Harvard 1869–1909. His elective system was directly related to the adoption of credits, though Professor Gerhard points out that he and his associates "had the best intention to lay the basis for individual growth." The need to find a common standard for high school work was also consequential. In addition, the credit system preserved flexibility while maintaining uniformity; permitted movement from one college to another; and reflected the application of business principles to mass education. Like many professors, Professor Gerhard dislikes the assigning of credit and the philosophy it implies:

> . . . the credit system . . . has an origin and meaning of its own. This is not a problem of old against new; of traditional, rigid, classical against modern, flexible, elective, though both then and now many will be inclined to interpret the development in such a way. In my opinion, it is a case of the means defeating the end, of our giving preference to form over content, no matter what this content is.[5]

The tart critics of American higher education, like Thorstein Veblen and Abbott Lowell, were even harsher in their criticisms of forty years ago. Veblen, writing before 1918 against the system of academic grading and credit, called attention to "the pervasive way in which it resistlessly bends more and more of current instruction to its mechanical tests and progressively sterilizes all personal initiative and ambition that comes within its sweep."[6] Its acceptance today does not change the fact that only an educational system grown large and impersonal and remote from learning would tolerate it. Like all bureaucratic growths, it remains because, like weeds in hard soil, it cannot be pulled out without destroying the plants around it. The students can be blamed only in the abstract. Were they more avid for learning than students ever are, the elaborate formalization of the universities would not be necessary. As it is, they accept the bureaucracy and the tangible evidences of learning it so willingly provides.

College faculties speak often against the bureaucracy and even against the credit system. They dislike filling out forms, computing grades, assigning tests, registering students. But like an intellectual's avowed dislike for intellectuals, their dislike is not genuine. Teaching is a dreadfully unrevealing occupation. A teacher is hardly more aware of what he is sending out than of what the student is taking in. Denied the computable evidence that learning is taking place, the university professor would be more reluctant to teach than he is now. When his mind is off somewhere else, having heads to count and grades to assign assures him that he is meeting his teaching obligation. When his mind is on his teaching, he can feel superior to the academic bookkeeping going on all around him. At any time, he can furnish the solid particulars of teaching load to justify his pay: 6 hours of lecture $\times$ 3 = 18, + 4 hours of seminar $\times$ 4 = 16, + 3 hours of committee work, + 3 hours of miscellaneous add up to the 40 hours which assure everyone society is being served.

College professors want to be independent practitioners of the arts or skills or sciences they profess. They want to be known as historians or philologists or chemists whose excellence gives them independence. Most realize, however, that it is the routine of teaching, the credit hours handled, the students met, which afford the security of being a salaried employee. In the run of American institutions, where faculty members are dubiously expert, somewhat insecure, and not very confident about their right to lead the detached intellectual life, the bureaucracy provides an ideal government. It processes the student, provides written evidence of his progress, and dispels the professor's uneasy feeling that he is getting paid for indulging his personal inclinations.

As Robert M. Hutchins said long ago, "academic communities, whatever their protestations to the contrary, really prefer anarchy to any form of government." [7] What the individual professor wants is autonomy without responsibility, an orderly anarchy where someone in the business office keeps track of the retirement fund and gets his check out on time. The faculty finds this union of security with freedom in departmental organization, where self-interest can flower into departmental autonomy. For that, he is willing to put up with the bureaucracy, to submit to the regulations which are necessary for the department's health, as long as these regulations don't threaten *his* special course, *his* habits of work, *his* research projects. Like a hen in a brooder house, the scholar knows he can't be questioned about the egg he is hatching as long as he sits on the nest. By a show of active loyalty to his department, the faculty member preserves a distant connection with the larger purposes of the university without taking much of his time or enlarging his vision. Divided into dozens of petty kingdoms, the universities try to maintain sweetness if not light by building the academic honeycomb thicker and stickier.

Despite their expressed distaste for administration, faculty members find it difficult to leave administrative details to someone else. The widespread feeling that college presidencies are occupied by businessmen, politicians, lawyers, preachers, and rogues does not change the fact that by far the majority of presidents come from the academic ranks.[8] A large number hold Ph.D. degrees. Virtually all deans were once members of the teaching faculty. For an academic man, direct authority from an outsider is unthinkable. It must come from a member of the faculty who in time will become part of the faceless but imposing machinery called administration.

Because of the professor's penchant for letting George do it but wanting George to be a reasonably close copy of himself, the men who become department heads, or deans, or who are otherwise pulled into administration are those who reluctantly put scholarship aside, briefly or forever. Those who stay within the teaching or research faculty begin to feel a superiority about their own position. Administration, they say, is the dirty work. A first-rate clerk could handle most of it. If it pays more, it is only because the administrators are closer to the funds. Its financial gains are at the price of intellectual loss. The boys on the administrative ladder are those who weren't serious scholars in the first place, the opportunists who sensed the quickest way up, the ones incapable of the rigors of scholarship.

Faculty members turned into administrators are sensitive to these undercurrents of feeling, for they come close to being their own. Though they have local prominence, a higher salary, a gratifying feeling of power, and may be employing their talents in the best possible way, they count for less in the world of scholarship. They look back with longing to the classroom and the laboratory, to the old bibliographies in which their names still appear, to active membership in professional societies. When they die, where are the books and monographs which will take their names to generations of graduate students? However brilliant a scholar an administrator may have been, his administrative excellence is of a different kind from his scholarly fame. The suspicion develops that administrators are not only "different from" but "inferior to" the faculty. A dean, as the saying goes, is a man too smart to be president and not smart enough to be a professor. Such feelings help explain the change that takes place when faculty members become administrators. The same energies which might have enlarged the scholarly mind turn to enlarging the academic machine.

The full development of the administrator does not come until he begins to identify himself more with the public than with the faculty, when he eats more Rotary Club lunches than faculty breakfasts. The public has never been willing to let the universities alone. The reasons go back to the origin of American university government and forward to the persistent distrust of the democratic institutions in which the public takes such pride. Very early, American colleges and universities placed the highest level of control in the hands of boards of laymen. Conditions in the colonies did not permit a direct transplantation of an Oxford or a Cambridge. The fear of unorthodoxy, the absence of a strong body of learned men, the specific needs which the early college had to satisfy are some of the reasons that the English tradition of a minimum of government—and that under faculty control—did not pertain to American colleges. Instead, American colleges developed an administrative structure which was basically autocratic. Statutory control rested with the Board of Trustees, but since this board was a lay board and a nonresident one, actual control was vested in an executive appointed by the trustees, the president.

As long as a college was small and the branches of instruction few, the president had a fair chance, if he chose, of being an executive officer acting for the trustees and carrying out the wishes of the faculty. Or, as often happened, he could become the autocratic head of a family corporation. The autocratic pattern of control tended to concentrate power and consolidate functions. As presidents relinquished some of their powers, executive offices and officers multiplied, as did faculty functions and functionaries. The result is the dominant pattern of university government today: a self-nourishing bureaucracy in which everyone is entangled.

To help the members of the academic community find their way about, a corps of management experts has been brought in. The first principle of management is that there must be something to manage. Even when it conceals its identity under such names as the Bureau for Institutional Research or the Office of Coordinated Services, professional management is at its work of enlarging the operation. It deals in student stations in the library, and peak flow in the cafeterias, and profit and loss in the bookstores, and, of late, classroom space utilization. It sends out memos about communication up, communication down, and on the dead level. Its services often prove valuable, but always at the price of increasing the power of officialdom, the standardization of routines, and the number of individuals on campus not directly involved in learning.

The ratio of professional administrative personnel to academic personnel has risen strikingly. According to an Office of Education survey, "from the fall of 1955 to the fall of 1957, among all types of faculty and other professional staff positions, the largest proportionate increases were reported in the staff for general administration, 30%; staff for organized research, 20.2%; faculty for resident instruction in degree-credit courses, 13.4%." [9] This disproportionate increase is likely to continue as administrations try to stretch the supply of faculty by turning to efficiency. In management's desire to be helpful, the number of nonacademic personnel—already large because of the wide range of services—may grow larger still. Secretarial services are a case in point. What faculty member can resist the notion that high-salaried faculty members should not be doing the clerical tasks that low-salaried stenographers can do? Management's dream of a faculty office building with its pool of secretaries, its battery of dictaphones, is one the faculty can share. But secretaries not only perform busy work, they must be kept busy. They must be managed, their time cards filled out, and their employment forms filled in. Secretaries are as necessary to modern enterprise as Verifax machines, but higher education is not likely to get better by the simple multiplication of either.

Not the least of the offices at the executive level are those of the public relations men who try to keep the university in the public eye and at the same time free from criticism. Like their counterparts in industry, they too talk of the academic "image," the "package," and the "product." Their most useful service is erecting a barrier of office doors between the public and the president. A university president is uniquely accessible to the public. A parent who wouldn't think of writing a corporation president about her nineteen-year-old son's prospects for promotion will charge into a university president's office and demand that her nineteen-year-old son be protected from smutty talk in the washrooms. "Much of my time," a university president recently told his faculty, "is spent explaining a few of you." At best, allaying such suspicions consumes time and personnel. At worst, such suspicions lead to the demand for loyalty oaths or for the firing of professors for loose talk in the classrooms.

Suspicious or not, the public likes the show of enterprise. The president's official car is not merely for transportation. Quite apart from the needs of the institution, the chief executive needs to maintain an establishment, just as he needs an executive suite and a presidential assistant. The job of a university president is an onerous one, and no one would begrudge him enjoying the appurtenances of office that the public seems to think he should have. Nor can the university be blamed for accepting the comforts the public expects to find in institutions of higher learning.

In return, the universities feel obliged to keep expanding the range of services offered the public. Public entertainment is but one aspect; the range of community services now includes a survey service to fix the need for more services. Faculties have been as receptive as administrators to starting centers, institutes, bureaus, seminars, and groupings. The casual practice of speaking before community groups develops into a Speakers' Bureau. An afternoon discussion of the last election becomes a Seminar in American Politics. A social hour with foreign students becomes an Institute of International Relations. An outbreak of juvenile delinquency inaugurates the Bureau of Applied Social Dynamics. Each addition drags with it the machines, the personnel, the paperwork which swell the bureaucracy.

Within the faculty's domain, the professor's natural penchant for teaching only those things he precisely knows is strengthened by the public's desire to have him teach everything it wants to know. University administrations commonly blame the faculty for the proliferation of courses, which has kept pace with the proliferation of men and machines. Looked at closely, the large growth in courses is more attributable to the public's desire working itself into the curriculum. At my university in the past fifteen years, the multiplication of courses in traditional disciplines has been modest. Despite a greatly expanded graduate program, English offers no more courses now than it did in 1946; chemistry has expanded as might be expected from 36 to 64; economics from 40 to 75. In contrast, marketing and management have grown from 65 to 200; educational administration from 15 to 47; health, physical education, and recreation from 98 to 187. All of the latter increases are in areas where public desire has been as potent a force as subscholarly zeal.

Driver education is a specific example. It first appeared on the Utah campus one summer as a special course offered by a visiting expert through the Extension Division. A year later, it had become a part of the regular curriculum. The following year, it had grown into a proposed minor in Driver and Safety Education and was being offered to the Faculty Council for approval. The twenty-one credit hours included required courses in Prevention and Emergency Care of Injuries, Safety Education, Driver Education, Special Problems in Driver Education, and a choice of electives from among Red Cross First Aid Instructor's Course, Survey of Audiovisual Materials, Camping, The Alcohol Problem and Education, and Individual Study and Research. The Council approved the program by one vote. At this point, a little-used faculty regulation which provides for a review of Faculty Council actions by the entire faculty subjected the proposed minor to further debate. The minor in driver education was defeated. Whether that was any substantial victory may be judged by examining the full description of Driver Education courses as they now appear in the university catalogue. Regardless of academic scruples, the public is having its way.

150. Driver and Traffic Education. Su A S (5)
For prospective teachers of driver education. Classroom and behind-the-wheel instruction; knowledge, attitudes, and skills; trainee experience in teaching non-drivers; three classroom and four laboratory periods per week. Register in the Extension Division.

151. Driver Education. W Su (4)
Personality factors of the driver, simulators, car care, relations with administrators and support agencies, special driving techniques, and evaluation of aids. Prerequisite: Health Education 143 and 150. Register in the Extension Division.

154. Special Problems in Driver Education. W (4)
Relationships of driver education to the vital field of enforcement; relations to local, county, and state police; adult and juvenile courts; driver license bureau; effects of stimulants and depressants; traffic engineering. Prerequisite: Health Education 151. Register in the Extension Division.

The consequences of the academic bureaucracy are both trivial and consequential, trivial in the inanities of the curriculum, the pettiness of routines, the accretions of habit; consequential in the effects that trivial abuses have in lowering the tone of academic life. The hard questions are these: How inclusive of men's skills, arts, and knowledge can the university become without losing the power to discriminate between things of little and much worth? How far can the university go to facilitate learning before the means become superior to the ends? How far can the university extend choice and flexibility without impairing the discipline of learning?

Beyond these particular questions is the large question of whether the university can so rule itself as to preserve principles and define high policies and practices. Administrations are what they are—swollen in size, assertive of authority, enamored of machines, projects and growth—because the academic community has failed to produce anything better. Faculty senates and councils have proved as fond of electing the safe candidates, of interminable debate, of tabled motions and deferred action as any other bureaucratic body. Neither the students nor the trustees have the direct and continuing involvement in university life that would make them the directing force in university government.

Faculty senates, for all their torpor, are the active parts of the faculty bodies. The small number who serve are those within the faculty who are interested in over-all university policy. A somewhat smaller number of these are actively interested in higher education apart from their own campus. The rest are tethered to disciplines, fenced off within departments, caught between students and administration as the administration is caught between the faculty and the public. Many of the older professors, having fought too many real and imaginary battles, have quietly withdrawn. The young men on the scholarly make have little time for the making of policy. The sociologists know there is no sense in fighting institutional accretions. The humanists preach discretion as the better part of valor. The philosophers see clearly that all is vanity except, perhaps, symbolic logic.

At its worst, the difficulty of achieving order in an inherently disorderly house results in the melancholy events which blighted the University of Nevada from 1952 to 1956. The central issue came to be the violation of academic freedom and tenure arising from a new president's move to discharge five members of the faculty. The central fight was between a professor jealous of his rights and an autocratic administrator jealous of his power. Behind that fight was the broader conflict between the classical liberal arts philosophy of many members of the faculty and the American public schools philosophy of the president. The argument reached the public in the question of whether a state university can have standards of admission. It affected the students to the degree that many began seriously questioning the kind of education that they were receiving.

The entangled and often conflicting interests of public, students, faculty, and trustees lie behind the dramatic confrontation of President Stout and Professor Frank Richardson at the climax of the Nevada controversy. As it appeared in the stenographic report, the conclusion of the interview went like this:

STOUT: Aren't there some unsolved problems in the field of biology that would keep you busy, and leave other problems to other people?

RICHARDSON: I have to be concerned with admission requirements. I am interested in my own children's education and the students in my classes.

STOUT: Frankly, it is none of your business. That rests in the hands of the regents.

RICHARDSON: It does affect me in many ways, however, the quality of students and their attitudes. I am necessarily concerned.

STOUT: We are not going into that discussion because, as I said, you are hired to teach biology and not to be a buttinsky all over the campus. Dean Wood is responsible for all of the college of liberal arts. I have confidence that he can handle that. If you handle the department of biology as it should be handled, I think you will have your hands full. Otherwise, Mr. Richardson, something else will have to be done. I may be a little more blunt than some people have been in the past but I think certain things have been pointed out to you in the past and I just don't believe in fooling around. If you are not happy in the job that is assigned to you, we will help you move, but as long as you stay here, we will ask you for help in other areas when we need it. That is all. Do you have anything to say, Dean Wood?

WOOD: No.[10]

Ultimately, the Supreme Court of Nevada ordered reinstatement of Professor Richardson. As an aftermath of the struggle, an objective appraisal of the university was ordered by the Nevada Legislative Commission. The appraisal team's report was published in 1957. It is a remarkable document which not only discloses the complex situation at the University of Nevada but the complexities of running any American university. The main issue as defined by one member of the appraisal team is one of the main issues of academic bureaucracy: "subject matter, ideas, and professional standards versus techniques, getting adjusted and being liked, and the wishes of the public." [11]

Since 1957, the damage to the University of Nevada has been slowly repaired. A new president has been installed. Blame and praise have been apportioned all around. If there is any general satisfaction to be gained from the events, it is the knowledge that, ugly as the confrontation often was, it disclosed the presence of personal forces vitally interested in the higher purposes of the university. In many institutions where the bureaucratic hum muffles the voices of contention, no one can be sure anyone is directing the academic enterprise.

PART THREE

Problems

8. The Fourth R

NOT long ago, a freshman student walked up to my table at registration in a medium-sized university and asked, with no particular note of embarrassment, "Say, where do you sign up for dumbbell English?" Being an English teacher, I could tell him, and I did. Later that year, I was talking to a textbook salesman who referred in the same matter-of-fact way to "bonehead" courses. His company was preparing some new material in "bonehead," he told me; big demand for it, especially in English and mathematics. Coming as they did from sources keenly sensitive to changing academic fashion, these two remarks indicated to me that the "dumbbell" course had become an accepted part of the university program.

"Dumbbell" and "bonehead" are unacademic but unequivocal terms for what college catalogues describe as "remedial" courses, courses designed to remedy deficiencies which students possess when they enter college. Although remedial courses are nothing new to the college curriculum, in the past they have not occupied a large place, even in departments teaching basic skills. But in recent years in many colleges, more and more of the faculty's time has been devoted to meeting the needs of entering freshmen who read badly, write poorly, and figure inaccurately, if at all. The problem of the deficient student is one that appears at all levels of American education. With the greatly expanding college enrollments, it promises to become one of the major problems of higher education.

Here there will be no attempt to blame the elementary and secondary schools for all the deficiencies in college freshmen. That rationalization has too long provided an easy out for unthinking defenders of higher education, and a proof of inadequacy for all those who know what is wrong with the public schools. What should become increasingly apparent in the future is that the responsibility for dealing with the deficient student is one which all levels of education must share. The public school teacher has always had to work with the dullard; it is only recently that the college professor has had to face a somewhat similar chore.

It should also be noted that although the problem of taking care of the deficient student is a large one nationally, it coexists, rather paradoxically, with the fact that many of the country's better private schools are turning away increasing numbers of highly qualified applicants. Admissions directors in such schools can resist, to a great extent, the pressure of numbers and take only the very top students. But publicly supported universities, and many private colleges operating with small endowments and necessarily maintaining close relationships with their immediate communities, have little choice. The students, good and bad, are asking to get in, and public sentiment is strongly against the exclusion of any great number of those who have the money and the desire to go to college.

Some figures gathered from around the country will indicate the magnitude of the problem. At the University of Illinois in 1956, 954 freshmen or 29.8 per cent of the first-year class were taking the remedial English course. At Ohio State, of 4,479 students taking the mathematics placement test, 1,529 qualified for regular mathematics; 887 for Mathematics 401, a remedial course; and 1,071 for Mathematics 400, described as a preremedial course. At Ohio University, a study of remedial English in 1949 disclosed that 25.3 per cent of the freshman class were enrolled in remedial sections. A survey of ten state schools in the Rocky Mountain area revealed that some kind of remedial program was being given in all the schools, with the number of students involved ranging from 10 to 30 per cent of the freshmen enrolled.

Most of the above figures were compiled in the midfifties, a time which may prove to be the high-water mark of remedial instruction. Since then, colleges and universities have become more hard-boiled about permitting remedial classes to become a part of the university program.[1] A good many have discontinued remedial classes altogether, and the poor student must take his chances with the good student from the beginning. Other schools have put remedial work into the extension division, oftentimes charging an extra fee. Still others have disguised such subcollege work as clinics or workshops which offer help in addition to regular classes. This show of strictness has cut down somewhat on the number of students requiring remedial instruction. Many of the poorest risks may have decided not to fight the odds; others have found the demands of the preadmission remedial classes too great. Some, of course, have transferred their applications to schools which cut their standards to meet the capacities of the applicants.

But though the number of inadequately prepared students being admitted to college may have decreased, the growing assumption that everyone goes on to college will bring to the universities in the next decade a great many students poorly equipped with the basic skills of reading, writing, and arithmetic. What this means for the individual student is that he reads with difficulty, writes hardly at all, and figures only in round numbers. What it means for the college teacher in the basic skills is that a large part of his energy is taken up with remedial work, what he may think of, in moments of despair, as the fourth R. The wasted energies, the daily frustrations, the personal conflicts of both student and teacher are the obvious and distressing consequences of the remedial program.

There are students in these classes, of course, who are actually suffering from inadequate past training; or from lack of attention in high school; or from freshman football, social activities, maladjustment, or laziness. Without question, remedial help is of some value to such students. Unfortunately, the remedial courses handle a relatively small number of them. Principally, the courses are concerned with the large group of students who just cannot comprehend, whose basic mental equipment is not up to the particular demands placed upon it.

Faced with this kind of deficient student, the teacher's immediate concern is personal and somewhat removed from his philosophical attitude toward the problem in the abstract, for he finds himself involved in the personal relationships which always exist between a teacher and the students who are doomed to fail. An intense discomfort arises from not quite being able to talk to them with the proper blend of charity, pious hope, and impersonal firmness. After an extended session with one of these students—students who are as often as not sincere, conscientious, personable, and hard-working, and who, for all this, still cannot fashion an English sentence or master a simple equation—a teacher gets the dismaying feeling that nothing can be done. At such times, he may regret the absence from our culture of an intellectual Charles Atlas, a pedagogue who could advertise on the back pages of middlebrow magazines a course designed to change 98 I.Q. weaklings into 200 I.Q. dynamos. One can picture, in his fancies, a lad formerly much put upon by young men with high foreheads and horn-rimmed glasses, suddenly repossessing the girl of his intellectual dreams with his knowledge of the periphrastic subjunctive. But these are fancies. Whatever it may be possible to do with human material in terms of personality development and character building, there has been limited success in injecting basic intelligence into failing college students.

It is not a pleasant fact to face. Educators have been affirming and denying its implications for centuries. And every time one of the perpetual freshmen in the remedial course faces the teacher, the problem objectifies and humanizes itself. It is not easy to say, "You are failing, sir, and would be better off elsewhere," no matter what terms one uses. Even for an English teacher it is not easy to find euphemisms and syntax which turn this basic and brutal sentence into "adjustment of one's fundamental capacities to no less commendable but more achievable goals." And yet, there seems to be little kindness in holding out next quarter, next term, next year, as the one in which the poor struggler's abilities will miraculously match a subject's complexities. Once the student is admitted to the university, it too often becomes the necessity for the teacher to smuggle the unpleasant facts of human inability into the student's consciousness.

The success of students in remedial programs is not great. Two similar studies, one at the State College of Washington and the other at Ohio University, showed that about 20 to 25 per cent of those enrolled in remedial English were eventually graduated as compared with about 40 per cent for the rest of the freshman class.[2] At Ohio State, 344 of 894 students taking remedial English failed the course, and 90 per cent of these failed out of the University. Of 137 students at the University of Utah in 1958 who were informed that they must take remedial courses, fifteen were still enrolled in the university in the fall of 1960, and only three of these had a cumulative average above C. The same fall at Utah, 54 per cent of 95 students passed remedial reading the first time through; 50 per cent of 197 passed remedial English; and 36 per cent of 321 passed remedial mathematics.

The content of remedial courses may be inferred from these questions, taken from the final examination in remedial mathematics at a state university:

15. A recipe requires 1¾ cups of sugar. How much sugar will be needed to make 3½ times this recipe?
16. If John buys pencils at the rate of 3 pencils for 12 cents and sells them to his classmates at 5 cents each, his profit on the sale of 36 pencils is ________ cents.
29. Solve for s: $P = 2s + 2w$.
35. Find the area of a rectangle 38 in. × 3.4 feet.
42. A car travels 66 feet per second. Find its speed in miles per hour.
49. Subtract 8 gallons 2 quarts 1 pint from 19 gallons.

The accomplishments of remedial students in English are evidenced in this example of a final theme, reprinted exactly as written:

Yes, I have made a really close friend since I came to college. His name is Jhon S________ he is from D________, Ohio. The first time we meate, was the first weak of school. Because both of use live in the same house. He is not my room mate, But he live just across the hall with a Boy from S________, Ohio. Jhon and I ride home ever week together. One week he drive and the other week I drive. We go every place to gether around campus. If one of us have a date we try to get the other a date too. So as you can see this is just more than a really close friend ship.

When we goth go home we try to go som place together if it is only to a show or to the bowling alleys.

You might think we both live in the same town but you are worng. Jhon lived in D________ and I live in C________, Ohio. The towns are about three to four miles apart. But we never mate before the first week of school.[3]

The expense and the waste which accompany such records of nonachievement are obvious. Dissatisfaction with the results achieved is a major reason why many universities have discontinued remedial work.[4]

The burden of these remedial courses is onerous and unrewarding and frustrating because they cannot be wished out of existence any more than basic intelligence can be wished into being. There is no easy solution—for the teacher, for the administrator, and, most pathetic of all, for the "bonehead" himself. The problem is, among other things, an intensely human one and deserves to be seen in its human terms; but it is also a rather concrete manifestation of certain abstract and general problems facing higher education in the United States, and must be looked at in its larger context.

The remedial program is a reflection of the basic issue in American education: the urge to educate to a high degree the entire populace and the difficulties of doing it. Looked at in this way, the "burden of bonehead" may have been brought upon higher education by the educators themselves in selling the public, if not precisely on higher education, at least upon the practical and social advantages of a college degree. The selling has not been hypocritical—a degree, whatever its inadequacy as the measure of an educated man, has job value and snob value. One cannot blame the college freshman for failing to appreciate the subtle but great difference between the practical advantages of attending college and the actual attending.

From this kind of public attitude (a kind of abstract recognition granted to a profession denied more concrete manifestations of public support and esteem), the pressures go forth to university controlling bodies to deny no one the opportunity of attending publicly supported schools. Indirectly, because of the large part public institutions play in higher education (over one-half of the current enrollment is in publicly supported colleges and universities), and because of the general demand for "degreeified" people, private schools feel the same pressures. Economically, too, the impoverished private school finds it hard to turn away those who can put up the necessary tuition. Thus, directly and indirectly, socially and economically, many of our colleges and universities are under great pressure to keep admissions policies as liberal as possible.

Then, too, there is the great pressure of the democratic ideal which finds the distinction between equality of intellect and equality of opportunity hard to mark. How strong this pressure is, not just among the vast majority of voting Americans but among people with some interest and experience in higher education, can be measured by the responses to an article titled "Education for All Is Education for None," which appeared in the *New York Times Magazine* a half-dozen years ago. It was written by Douglas Bush, professor of English at Harvard and a respected scholar both here and abroad. Mr. Bush met the issue squarely when he wrote, ". . . I see no reason why the flood of students should be allowed to pour into college, why automatic graduation from school should qualify anyone for admission." [5]

The merits of such a stand are considerable, and if future enrollments are as large as predicted, partial acceptance of such a view may well be inescapable. But, setting aside the merits or weaknesses of the argument, what is of interest is the strength and nature of the replies. The *Times* reported that responses ran 4 to 1 against Mr. Bush.[6] Moreover, from the samples printed, many of the replies were heated and injudicious. An English professor at Cornell cited the writer's "Piltdown philosophy." A man from New York City called his view "the worst type of snobbery" and his mind "a mind . . . essentially fascistic." A professor of education found "triteness of . . . content" and "lack . . . of thoughtful and responsible treatment."

Such responses coming from what one might fairly judge to be a well educated audience indicates that it is still close to impossible to mention inequality of intellect and not be charged with snobbery and lack of faith in democratic ideals. The question Mr. Bush raised with a wider audience is one with which professional educators have long been concerned: "Who should go to college?" For the educator as for the layman, the American belief in the economic and social benefits of higher education and the American suspicion toward education at any level which takes some and excludes others complicate discussion of the question.

But if there is disagreement about who should be given higher education, there is rather wide agreement about who can successfully complete the four-year college program. The top one-fourth of the college-age group, roughly corresponding to those with intelligence quotients of 110 or above, is most often cited as the group with a reasonable chance of mastering the four-year college program. Byron S. Hollinshead, while president of Coe College, studied the problem thoroughly for the Commission on Financing Higher Education in 1950. He concluded that the mark —100 intelligence quotient—was the point below which the student became a "calculated risk," where his chance of finishing college successfully dropped below 50-50.[7] Such a figure is, of course, an approximation, but an approximation based upon considerable observation of what happens to students below and above this level when they attend college. Commenting upon this figure, Mr. Hollinshead wrote, "Where the borderlines are to be drawn depends on the calculated risks the individual, the college, and society are willing to take."

With the strong currents for higher education for all in America, the risks the individual, and society, and to a degree, the college take are bound to be large. The size of the remedial programs and the increasing enrollments are evidences that the risks are already being taken. There is every indication that the proportion of citizens going on to college will continue to increase. When one reflects that of the upper one-fourth who are regarded as having a reasonable chance for success in college, only about one-half ever attend, one gets an idea of the number of those who are not particularly well equipped who are filling the classrooms.

Probably between one-third and one-half of the freshman enrollment could be objectively regarded as good risks in the four-year college.

The increasing enrollments during the next decade make an increase in the number of deficient students almost certain. The pressures from increased enrollments are likely to force admissions standards up somewhat. Where walls cannot be moved, buildings built, teachers hired, class sizes increased, funds stretched, colleges will have to impose limitations upon the number of students admitted, and these limitations will be applied to the less able or the poorly prepared. But public pressures will force many colleges—if not the large private schools, certainly the publicly supported ones—to expand to meet enrollments. In general, professional sentiment at the present time seems to be toward expansion rather than limitation. With such expansion, the problem of what to do with the deficient student, as well as most other college problems, will become larger but no easier to solve.

The "real problem," wrote Ordway Tead in 1956, ". . . is not either quantity or quality as now conceived. It is both the salvaging and enhancing of quality and at the same time the eager acceptance of quantity as an imperative democratic mandate."[8] Such a statement implies a necessary reassessment of higher education, particularly of its organization and objectives. Certainly it is a fair assumption that the kind of higher education which served a student body of 239,000 comprising 4 per cent of the college-age population, is not likely to be equally suited to a student body which now numbers over four million and which comprises at least 22 per cent. Yet this is the bare numerical difference between the college population of 1900 and that of today. The figures do not begin to suggest the differences between the demands, needs, and ideals of both the individual and the society at one period of time as compared with the other; but, although there have been some changes in emphasis, in the nature of the curriculum, in professional training, in facilities and equipment, the basic pattern of the four-year program has not markedly changed.

The discrepancy between a relatively unchanged college program with its traditional standards and a vastly changed student body both in number and abilities does much to explain the increasing number of students that colleges deem deficient. Committed to an old academic tradition and organized to fulfill these ideals, yet faced with educating quite unacademic multitudes, the colleges are not doing as well as they might by either the superior students or the deficient ones. The "eggheads" and the "boneheads" are inextricably mixed, and the results are about what one can imagine.

The obvious solution of raising standards and keeping the dullards out is really no more satisfactory than one which dispenses with standards and adapts to the lowest common denominator. What is needed to begin with is the drawing of a distinction between the kind of higher education which the Bachelor of Arts degree once represented and which, by and large, colleges still try to preserve, and the kind of higher education which can be profitable to those who are not up to the traditional four-year program but who are still capable of mastering some kind of useful training beyond high school.

This is not a new idea. The President's Commission on Higher Education in 1947 drew a distinction between the 49 per cent it thought were capable of completing fourteen years of schooling and the 32 per cent which might profitably complete a more advanced liberal or professional program. Two-year terminal programs within the four-year college, the granting of special certificates of various kinds, the spread of junior colleges and community colleges—these are evidences that the degree-granting institutions have recognized the distinction and have tried to do something about it.[9]

Colleges must go further and must act vigorously to effect an actual separation between the degree-granting college restricted to students of real ability and a new kind of college, perhaps an extension of the junior college as now constituted—a college designed for the less academically capable but still one which offers a program of substantial worth.[10] The alternative is to proceed with the present rather general practice of watering down the B.A. program by adjusting the curriculum, lowering the standards, grading by attendance and the IBM machine, in order to accommodate all ranges of student abilities.

Such a separation should improve the opportunities for the gifted as well as for the less capable. Lack of motivation is one of the chief reasons why about one-half of the superior one-fourth of the college-age youth do not go on to college.[11] While initial motivation must chiefly come from outside the university, the character of higher education does much to shape the prospective student's attitude toward it. The kind of college which clearly fulfills the purposes of stimulating, guiding, and honoring intellectual endeavor should increase the motivation of the capable student who is undecided about his future plans. Once in college, he should find the kind of challenging atmosphere which would keep him there and permit his fullest development. At the same time, the less capable student would not be subjected to the pattern of repeated failure now characteristic of the remedial program. He, too, would find that within his limitations he could have a similarly enriching post-high school experience in learning.

One might question that the public would accept separation of publicly supported institutions into those for the good students and those for the poor ones. Were such a separation proposed in precisely these terms and acted upon abruptly throughout the country, it would surely meet opposition; changes in education must proceed slowly. If this change were to come about, it would be a gradual development which took its impetus and direction from the colleges and which gained its adherents or opponents from the general public along the way.

Even now, colleges and universities do not exist in the mind of the public as institutions all of one color. The desire to send the children to a "better" school reflects an appraisal of the quality of the institution as well as a consideration of its social prestige. Graduate students are highly selective in deciding where to pursue an advanced degree, and the quality of the program offered is often decisive. The colleges and universities which the average citizen is likely to cite as the nation's best are similarly selective in choosing their students, and this selectivity in turn strengthens the impression of quality in the public mind. Such qualitative distinctions are already accepted, and it should not be impossible to gain public acceptance of a somewhat broader distinction between kinds of undergraduate schools.

Any marked physical separation of the kinds of colleges proposed is not likely to come at once, if at all. Existing facilities would doubtless have to continue taking care of a heterogeneous student group even though programs and faculties for such programs were to be sharply separated. Such separations already exist to a degree in the preprofessional programs, or in requirements for teacher's certificates as compared with the liberal-arts program, and in the graduate schools which share buildings and faculties with undergraduate colleges.

While it might be desirable, it would probably be difficult to have existing institutions or new colleges narrow their objectives to one kind of program or another. The colleges of Limbo, for example, would profit greatly if they would stop trying to compete with the largest and best universities in the land. But to do so, these colleges would have to scrap tradition, thoroughly reorganize the staff and the criteria for selecting staff, and accept a secondary role. Even were they willing to do all of these, they could still argue and with justice that students would not knowingly enroll in a college that gave an inferior degree.

This is the most difficult problem, for it involves changing attitudes of almost all those involved in higher education. One thing is certain. No more favorable climate for striking out in new directions could be found than in the next decade. The colleges will have a seller's market. The value of the B.A. and the B.S. degrees has already dropped and will probably drop further. An employer cannot have the reliance upon a college degree he may once have had. With a vastly increasing number of new jobs for which specific technical training is necessary, new college programs should find ready acceptance. The kind of college I am proposing would undoubtedly have a more vocational nature than the liberal arts college of today. Its graduates might not be as bright, but they might be more specifically and usefully trained. In time, a good college, carefully planned and staffed to meet limited but specific objectives, might win a following by the evidence of graduates ready to satisfy the specific needs of a technological society.

Meeting the cost of the country's expanding system of higher education will be difficult regardless of the kinds of colleges and universities which make up that system. There is little doubt of the ability of the country to meet the cost, though it is not likely that in the future funds will be any more generously distributed than they are now. It seems probable, however, that a system of higher education that ministered more exactly and adequately to the different intellectual capacities of its students would result in substantial savings of the country's human resources. Such savings would be hard to communicate to the public, but the individual citizen might at least gain a clearer idea of the extent and kind of higher education he can afford.

No one need take offense that society would be casting out the dullard. The situation is simply that higher education cannot afford to sacrifice those most capable of profiting from it because of taking care of a large portion for whom college is frustration on the installment plan. We need to do better by the "boneheads," and at the same time better by the more promising students who are neglected in our efforts to salvage the others.

9. Teaching

HIGHER education deals in ideas as banks do in money. American universities have never been sure that "ideas" are their stock in trade. And though American banks were once quite firm about money, they are now moving steadily in a direction which makes the analogy between banks and universities, money and ideas, instructive. As the British writer Malcolm Bradbury recently pointed out, American banks are not awed by money or even respectful toward it.[1] "The last thing an American banker would like you to think of him," Bradbury wrote, "is that he might *deal* in cash. He deals in bonds, and he finances things, but he doesn't touch money." Banks today are no more repositories of money than gas stations of gasoline. The purpose of both is to keep the product flowing, to extract a profit from the transactions, and to offer a flock of extra services that produce more income and more satisfaction than the mere handling of money or the pumping of gas. Both banks and gas stations expend their creative energies in devising ways to attract trade, not seeming to recognize that money and gas are the two things modern man cannot live without.

There are differences, however, between the bank and the gas station, on the one hand, and the university, on the other. The banker builds his confidence on the legal and moral certainty that the lending of money entails a suitable rate of return. The service station man is equally certain that what he puts in the tank is what makes the car go. The academic man has neither assurance; nor can he say, except in jest, "Madam, we guarantee satisfaction or we return the boy." He can, like the old-time banker in the days before the service station was born, maintain a hard stewardship over the funds, accumulate with zeal, pay out with reluctance, and get across the lesson that intellectual capital is difficult to acquire, hard to hold, and worthy of ritual and respect. Few academic men do. Instead, like managers of savings and loan establishments, they disparage the solemnities of saving and spending by promoting a universal spirit of ease and growth and fun.

Despite the outward show—the football, the sorority sings, the bowling alleys—and the inward doubts of professors and administrators, universities are concerned with ideas. They display their concern chiefly through teaching and research. The two struggle for primacy, teaching, as one might suspect, being more often honored in the abstract, and research more often rewarded in hard cash.

Teaching, which, like writing, generates new ideas in the act of formulating and transmitting existing ones, is a debased art in most colleges and universities. If it were practiced as it should be, it would engage the teacher in a wide range of ideas steadily and intensely day after day. As it is most frequently practiced, teaching is to ideas as fly-tying is to fishing. Both are personal, ritual skills which, once learned, can be performed idly and with a satisfaction quite unrelated either to engaging the students' minds or to catching fish. Teaching at its best is a great art, and great art of any kind is rare.[2] But the universities are not inclined to regard teaching as an art, or even as an occupation worthy of a teacher's full time and energy, or to encourage teaching that rises above a kind of middle level, that hits the students somewhat above where they sit down and well below where they think.

An excessive concern for research is customarily blamed for the neglect of teaching. The academic equation—scholarship equals research, research equals publication, publication equals success—is accepted even as it is preached against. "College Teachers Who Don't Teach," is the title of an article in the *New York Times Magazine* which connects the "heightened status of the researcher" with "the downgrading of the teacher."[3] "In fact," the writer claims, "to call a person a good teacher in many leading institutions today is more than damnation by faint praise; it has become almost an academic smear. . . . The observant teacher sees that he is never promoted to more teaching, *but always to less.*"

As with other marriages of convenience, the troubles between teaching and research probably began when they first set up housekeeping together. I have reserved discussion of that arrangment for the next chapter. Here, I wish to put research aside and consider the individual and institutional traits which force teaching into the role of the long-suffering partner.

Teaching may suffer most from being the one thing everyone in the university does—and does, for the most part, casually. Lectures can be canned and delivered, and except for the annoyance of arriving somewhat on time and with regularity, the professor need hardly disturb his more intense preoccupations. Somewhere within the mind of the academic man dwells the image of the thinking self engaged in the precise task which calls forth and answers to his full intellectual powers. Meanwhile, the other self goes around doing the tasks that teaching demands: meeting classes, preparing lectures, reading books, scribbling notes, filing papers. Much of this routine work has become dirty work, honest toil turned into drudgery from the habit of doing it with the mind idle or only partially engaged.

Few colleges and universities do enough to encourage the teacher to develop his teaching into the honest craft it should be or into the magnificent skill it can become. The teacher's masters are many. They include the university and its administrators, the deans and department heads, the students and the public, and the faculty member himself. Together, they often give the impression that they are suspicious or hostile toward teaching which deals sharply, provocatively, or even freshly with students and ideas. Such teaching, of course, can offend donors or scare legislators or upset students. But suspicion and hostility most often arise from nothing more sinister than the tendency of men in charge of any enterprise to think that the work is not getting done if the figures aren't coming in, the products going out, the hours being expended. Administrators can never be sure what is going on behind the closed door of classroom or study. Even the teacher leaving the classroom with his books and notes and ideas cannot be certain how valuable a transaction has just taken place.

Teaching, for all its endless verbalizing, is a silent, secret, submerged art. University teachers insist upon the sanctity of the classroom. Their communication within it is not with their peers or with the world outside. Today's doctor of philosophy has a very private practice, enclosed by the specialized courses he can call his own and protected from inquiry, scrutiny, and criticism by academic traditions and superstitions. Among these are beliefs that the Ph.D. is a license to teach; that scholarly assiduity ensures good teaching or makes up for bad; that the popular teacher can't be profound and the profound one popular; that learning is a dull business and that many professors prove it; that vitality enervates; that brilliance terrifies; that wit cheapens—in short that, depending on the way one looks at it, no teaching is bad teaching and even the worst teacher will be discovered by some student, some time, as very good indeed. Each of these premises can be defended vigorously. The effects of teaching are personal, slow to work, and slow to be discovered. Much of the effort goes immediately underground, some to germinate and to flower in unexpected ways. It is hardly easier to judge ultimate effects than to say which seed in a forest is to become a tree.

Of the teacher's three chief obligations—teaching, administration, and scholarship—teaching is the hardest to appraise. Though many studies have been made that attempt to evaluate teaching, college faculties tend to regard such attempts as hopeless, meddlesome, and illicit traffic with the devils of education.[4] Teaching remains the great unknown, the quantity which can balance any equation. If a man is a proved research scholar, then how he teaches, or if he teaches, counts for little. If he is unimpressive in research, but a good fellow nevertheless, his teaching can be given more weight. If he does little research and is disagreeable as well, then good teaching alone cannot save him. In the American university, that which cannot be evaluated is not likely to be valued. As a consequence, teaching is the professional duty most easily and most often set aside. The hours of classroom performance are protected from other faculty obligations. The hours that precede the classroom are not similarly protected, either from the university or from the professor himself. Committee attendance in most universities is mandatory, but not attendance at one's own desk at a fixed time to prepare for the classroom. A manuscript going to a national journal demands a high degree of polish—not so, the daily lecture before a class. Places on conference programs are never filled by substitutes—the substitute is in the classroom where filling in is easy.

Good teaching and poor teaching are not so much matters of good teachers and poor teachers but of teachers whose effectiveness varies as rewards and circumstances lead them to teach at the top of their ability or at the bottom. At no point in the college teacher's career are conditions particularly favorable to consistently first-rate performance. The beginning teacher is given too much teaching and too much elementary teaching for which his highly specialized graduate work has made him temperamentally unfit. The new Ph.D. or the instructor still working on a dissertation is the one who teaches two, three, or four sections of freshman composition, or a comparable amount of beginning foreign language, or the bonehead sections of college mathematics. The teaching of rudimentary courses is not demeaning in itself. It becomes so when the courses become standardized, cut off from scholarship, and diluted in content; the students massed and sectioned; and the teaching consigned to a subclass of the faculty.[5] Against such odds, a young instructor finds it hard to teach well. The vigor of youth, the challenge of new experience, and his closeness to the student may vanish before his teaching begins to draw fully upon his skill, knowledge, and desire.

The middle years should be the years of greatest teaching skill, but they are often the years of greatest distraction. They are the years of the first book or the first twenty-five articles or the shouldering of committee responsibilities. They are years of travel grants, of administrative assignments, of government contracts. They are the years of finding out the painful and necessary lessons of scholarship. They often fall short as years of great teaching because teaching does not provide the most solid basis for a career. A few years as a brilliant teacher are all the beginning scholar can afford, or his university accept. When a young professor without tenure gets ready to take a permanent place on the staff, he needs a more solid set of credentials. In our better universities, it is a common practice to provide a faculty member in his years between promise and fulfillment with time off for finishing a book or a project. But where is the university that would offer time off for reading, contemplation, planning, and practicing which had no other end than that of improving the teacher's skill?

Nor is excellent teaching necessarily to be found among the senior professors. In many ways, the senior professors have won the right to teach and have accumulated the skills and wisdom to teach to perfection. Nevertheless, much is against their doing so: their distance from the students; their development as specialized scholars; their drift into idiosyncrasy, fixed ways, and routine patterns of performance; their embarrassment at hearing thirty or forty years of the same voice going over the same ground. Dealing with ideas in the classroom requires receptivity, flexibility, and freshness of response. Men grow old, and teaching, more than scholarship itself, suffers from a lack of physical vigor.

The laboratory sciences aside, teaching in the universities is almost entirely verbal. The teacher who works with words must somehow, from raw particulars of fact through the workings of mind and heart and the expenditure of his skills, implant within the students' minds the basic truth that *thought* gives human life distinction. Whatever one teaches, that conviction must arrive with such force and so argue its worth that the student cannot remain the same. This highest kind of teaching is the university's particular responsibility and lies well beyond the mere transmission of fact, the demonstration of techniques, the disciplining of skills which occupy so much of the university's time.

Alfred North Whitehead, in that most remarkable of books about teaching, *The Aims of Education,* proceeds from the obvious fact that knowledge is a chief aim of intellectual education. But, he writes, "there is another ingredient, vaguer but greater, and more dominating in its importance. The ancients called it 'wisdom.' . . . The only avenue towards wisdom is by freedom in the presence of knowledge. But the only avenue towards knowledge is by discipline in the acquirement of ordered fact. Freedom and discipline are the two essentials of education." No college course in "methods" is likely to provide a sounder basis for teaching than Professor Whitehead's discussion of these basic principles.

Freedom and discipline. The principle of freedom demands that teaching must interest, excite, bring joy. It implies that teaching must be a performance, either the natural gift of the born actor or the calculated effects of the trained performer.

Without one or the other, learning is lost in the distance that separates the learner struggling with his rudimentary ideas from the teacher personally and intensely involved in ideas that lie beyond or tangential to these. In Professor Whitehead's words:

> Knowledge does not keep any better than fish. You may be dealing with knowledge of the old species, with some old truth; but somehow or other it must come to the students, as it were, just drawn out of the sea and with the freshness of its immediate importance.[6]

The "somehow or other" includes all the myriad intricacies of thought and performance by which a teacher engages a student's mind.

Gilbert Highet, Professor of Classics at Columbia University, is that rare example of superb teacher and scholar. His course, "Classical Influences in European Literature," was so genuinely exciting that students attending one year came back to hear it again the next. In returning, they discovered that what had seemed—and still seemed—so spontaneous was, in fact, a brilliantly executed performance. One could assume that the precise inflection, the illuminating anecdote, even gesture and pause were being repeated when they found response, sharpened or altered when they did not. Like an actor bringing to life a person long dead, Professor Highet brought ideas to life from dead fact. Few teachers possess such talent; their consolation is that there are many ways of catching the student's attention. What is most important is that the student must be caught, and the teacher must be the catcher.

The principle of discipline insists that teaching must make demands, and the student must answer to them. It implies the imposition of requirements and standards. The universities have sufficient discipline of a kind, and university teachers, who take on the coloring of their environment, seldom fall short in this respect. They have the official record book to fill with checks and letters and signs to attest that the student is being made to toe the mark. The more meaningful discipline which arises from a student's desire to master a subject and that subject's resistance to his efforts is less common. Mathematics is such a subject. The teaching of mathematics may fall short for want of life, but seldom for want of discipline. Precision, attention to detail, and the necessity of following a process through are conditions of successful performance. All courses in the exact sciences benefit from the nature of their demands. In the humanities, however, and especially in the social studies, the teacher often has to furnish the discipline which the study itself may not provide. In subjects still striving for exactness and pervaded with the spirit of vague social good will, discipline may not be present either in the subject or in the teaching of it.

The difference between one university subject and another with respect to discipline intensifies the university's need for a more unified course of study and for a more uniform set of practices. The skilled teacher can give his specialized subject the breadth which relates it to the broad pattern of learning and the strength which stretches the student's mind. The ordinary teacher does neither. He trusts that the routine lecture or the loose discussion will transmit knowledge and sets his standards by the objective examination. The almost universal neglect of writing as a part of university teaching keeps the student forever short of the self-discipline which marks the passage from the teacher teaching to the student learning.

Developing self-discipline—in teachers as in students—may be the whole difficulty. Human beings are always falling short. Escape from thought is a human failing. Thinking, in any exact sense of the word, is no more natural to man than walking erect. Man must putter. He must find something for hands, or feet, or mouth, or stomach to do. Life furnishes an endless supply of data, of raw figures to put down in rows and columns, within circles and squares, amidst arrows and asterisks. In his moments of pure thought, a man may see such activities for what they are—busywork to avoid facing ideas. "The devil finds work for idle hands," the proverb says, as if the devil were unconcerned with idle minds.

The academic man is not unique in this respect; where he differs from the mass of men is that his central task is thought—when he shirks it, this central task remains ill-done or undone. He is not even like the skilled surgeon whose skill of hand necessarily engages his brain at the moments when judgment must direct action. The humanist or the pure scientist has to seek out ties between action and thought. The physical act of teaching too rarely brings them forth; the unimpassioned act of investigation may be virtually mindless; the clash of mind with mind which is supposed to ring through the corridors is a duel with verbal swords, wrapped in abstractions. The condition is regrettable, like gravity, and no one is expected to surmount it except for brief and exhilarating moments. What is to be regretted most is that modern academic life conspires with the individual to make the complex acts of teaching and learning less than the great pleasures they should be.

10. Research

COLLEGES and universities display an uneasiness toward teaching which they do not display toward research. Even among those who become engaged in the debate between teaching and research, few urge that the prominence of research be diminished. Rather, teaching should be raised to the same level of prestige. The pretensions and practices of research are seldom questioned. Occasionally a member of an established discipline may scoff at a newcomer who begins to ape his methods—as English Ph.D.'s belittle graduate study in journalism, or future physicists speak disparagingly of engineers, or the whole liberal arts college shows disdain for colleges of education. But this is a mild kind of snobbery shown to any one trying to break into a fraternity. Indeed, it is in many of the new disciplines that research means the most. A research specialist in education today is worth his weight in public school administrators.

I have commented elsewhere that the ideals of "service" have not been able to dominate the university because of the presence of those traditional academic disciplines roughly defined as the liberal arts. These are the pure sciences—mathematics, physics, chemistry, biology, zoology, dedicated to the investigation of nature rather than the exploitation of it—and the humanities—language and literature, philosophy, history, tied to the study of man rather than the exploitation of him. Within the university, these two like to think of themselves as the thinking parts as contrasted with the other parts which perform grosser functions. Whether this attitude is just or unjust, the sciences and the humanities, broadly considered, encompass the world of learning. For that reason and because research in the universities is such a vast subject, this discussion leaves out much in order to concentrate on how the emphasis upon research affects university science and humanities.

The alliance between pure science and the humanities, like other alliances based on a mutual sense of superiority, has its inner conflict. Both the pure sciences and the humanities preach the highest academic ideals, but the one is listened to because it stands upon a mountain of material blessings which have transformed the world; the other is a mere creature of ideas, a purveyor of words, and with difficulty maintains the validity of its work.

This crucial difference is what divides C. P. Snow's "two cultures." The glory and the despair of science is that at its finest it has nothing to do with humans. A humanist, weary of past glories and despondent about future prospects of the human race, can only be envious. Nevertheless, among all the creatures in the universe, human beings alone seem concerned with ideas, and inquiries which set the human being aside may end up dealing with quantities not qualities, facts not words, things not ideas. These oppositions keep alive the quarrel between science and the humanities, but within the universities, the long series of skirmishes has depleted the ammunition on both sides. The opposing forces have withdrawn, not, as in most battles, each side claiming it has won, but rather both sides agreeing that the humanists have lost but each somewhat reluctant to advertise the fact.

Research in the sciences provides the pattern for graduate study which all departments of the university have accepted regardless of fit. Beyond the undergraduate level, no formal learning is possible that is not tied to extensive study in a limited area of knowledge somewhat arbitrarily defined by the existence of university departments and to a thesis "embodying the results of research, constituting a contribution to knowledge." In seventy-five years of graduate study, the only exception to this requirement has been the acceptance, in some areas of the humanities, of the "creative" thesis, which, in practice, has meant a labored effort to produce a creative version of the thing it sought to escape.

The validity of such a pattern of studies in the sciences is difficult to question. For the sciences, graduate education, both as preparation for a man entering the profession of college teaching and for one intending to devote himself to research, is excellent, at least in a technical way. Chiefly this is because research is what science is all about, and research is taught chiefly by practice and example. Overspecialization is an absurd charge to make against an intellectual enterprise which has won its way by specialization and which sees large by expanding human vision into the small. Nor can one seriously argue with the fundamental contention of the President's Science Advisory Committee that "the process of graduate education and the process of basic research *belong together* at every possible level." The relationship is described cogently in that committee's report:

> For as we are describing it, the process of graduate education depends on "research" just as much as upon "teaching"—indeed the two are essentially inseparable—and there is a radical error in trying to think of them as different or opposite forms of activity. From the point of view of the graduate student, the teaching and the research of his professor are, at the crucial point which defines the whole, united. What he learns is not opposite from research; it *is* research. Of course

many necessary parts of a scientist's education have little to do with research, and obviously also for many professors there must be a gap between teaching a standard graduate course and working at one's own problems. Moreover, many good teachers—men who keep up with the new work in their subject and communicate its meaning clearly to their students—are not themselves engaged in research. Yet we insist on the central point; the would-be scientist must learn what it is like to do science, and this, which is research, is the most important thing he can be "taught." [1]

How inappropriate this description is for the humanities can be demonstrated by substituting *humanities* for *science* in the last sentence of the paragraph. "The would-be humanist," it would read, "must learn what it is like to do humanities, and this, which is research, is the most important thing he can be 'taught.' " Humanists don't *do* humanities, and humanistic learning is *not* research, unless that term is expanded so far as to be meaningless. The humanist might go further and venture the guess that science and the research that is science can be trivial, and that the most laudable kind of advanced study in the sciences, as in the humanities, depends almost entirely upon wisdom and judgment.

Specialization and research as the universities now define them are not necessarily the highest attainments for the humanist. Knowledge which concerns itself with people and their ideas must be broad and it must be humane. But the feeling persists that if the humanities could be as exact, as receptive to technology, as efficient, as pure, as science, they would somehow strike closer to the truth and reap the rewards society now denies them. In some ways, the specialization in humanistic studies has been profitable. It has sharpened the humanist's critical insight; it has made scholarship more exacting; it has brought tools and techniques into the service of humanistic learning. On the other hand, it has encouraged the collection of facts, the assembling of data, without regard for the value of the subject or of the work involved in pursuing it. It has demanded an intensity of focus which too often kills the tissue of thought. It has ingrained patterns of routine investigation which keep the young scholar from thinking large and the seasoned scholar from encouraging him to do so. Often, it has atrophied the sensate being while sharpening the mind to the primitive utility of a pointed stick. In more tangible ways, it has filled the libraries with dissertations, stuffed the mailboxes with journals, and separated the learned man from the very humanity he supposedly studies.

What humanistic research modeled after science has accomplished appears in the volumes of published work which represent the highest intellectual strivings of America's most highly educated men and women. Creative and critical quarterlies, born of the mating of the pernicious inclination to write with the malignant necessity to publish, sponsor an incestuous scholarship in which the creative act of one succumbs to the analytical passion of the other.

Magazines of all kinds multiply at a startling rate. The Union List of New Serial Titles since 1949 is roughly half the size of the *complete* Union List of Serials to 1940. Those periodicals directly and even loosely connected with universities account for only a small proportion of this huge total, but it is reasonable to estimate that the number of scholarly periodicals has doubled in the past ten years. Bibliographies indicate the magnitude of academic publishing today. Check lists grow longer not only because of new publications but because of the scholar's penchant for neglecting nothing. In 1955, the Modern Language Association, the largest learned society concerned with the humanities, compiled its annual bibliography from 148 periodicals. In 1956, this list was expanded to include 1000 periodicals in eight languages. In American literature the number of publications being checked in 1950 was 84. The number now is about 375.

Jacques Barzun, Dean of Faculties and Provost of Columbia, gives an idea of what is in these journals and how it got there:

It is not as if the system required one to be a great scholar, or a good scholar, or even a scholar at all: it only requires that one *produce research*, which being translated means publish papers. Their contents should be in a certain form and they should be documented and if possible accurate—that is all. Thought, relevance to the interests of any other human being, engaging exposition or lucidity of prose are not mentioned among the specifications. The papers are merely asked for as evidence of professional discipline justifying one's existence—and promotion. And at the same time, "research" can be given as an excuse for neglecting the interests of the students or of the university.[2]

Pedantry, of course, has always been a danger to scholarship. It has seldom flourished as it does now, nor has its published form often before been the necessary qualification for academic employment and advancement.

The glut of publications has been accompanied by the development of a critical jargon as common to literature as to social science, and more disfiguring. Borrowing of terms from science has become the mark of the new critical preciosity. Many have by now become clichés. "Tension," "stasis," "fusion," "substrata," "extension," "catalyst," "pivotal," "dynamic," "subtend," "staticize," "polarize," "schematized," and "structured,"—these emerge from a casual leafing through a collection of literary essays. They appear in phrases like, "this aspect of the structure can be presented graphically," and "exposed the filaments of symbol," and "neither static and schematized nor wholly free and arbitrary, but contextual within a general framework."[3]

The development of an unfleshly vocabulary is matched by a prose style which loosely answers to Samuel Johnson's definition of a network: "reticulated or decussated at equal distances with interstices between the intersections." Thus, an essay begins, "We have frequently had occasion to note the difficulties of repetition or variation in literature on any extensive scale and to observe that these difficulties apply with particular force to any literary attempts at development of material by processes analagous to those of music."

Such a sentence is merely inept. It lacks the "density," to use a faddish critical term, and the "torsion," to create one of my own, of this example:

> Both Emerson and Thoreau, liberated from the authority of words as absolutely fixed terms, evolved a compensatory American theory of multiplicity, which resulted in linguistic media intended to delineate realities elusive of concrete linguistic definition.

A recent article in the academic journal, *College English,* takes English professors to task for writing this kind of prose and for the attitudes that encourage it. The author, John T. Flanagan, professor of English at Illinois, charges that a good many English teachers by "rigorous formalism" and "mechanical interpretation" drive students away from literature. Equally bad, he goes on, "so many of the monographs and studies written by teachers of the humanities are stylistically inept, stuffy, sodden."

Professor Flanagan's article aroused a puff of controversy which does not often enliven academic journals. Professor Roy Harvey Pearce called his criticisms unfair, and defended a literary scholar's occasional awkwardness of expression in attempting to "move beyond explication to a kind of philosophical criticism." [4] Bogged down in explication and analysis as it has been for the past twenty years, literary scholarship could afford to move beyond that sterile task. Few things are more revealing of the temper of literary criticism than *The Explicator,* a journal established in 1942 as "a clearinghouse for *explication de texte.*" One could guess that in literary studies the new criticism gained ascendancy over historical criticism just as the physical sciences became dominant among the natural sciences. As the original materials to be collected, annotated, and classified were exhausted, literary scholarship turned to the inexhaustible possibilities of critical analyses. The analogy with the natural sciences had at least placed emphasis upon the living organism; the analogy with the physical sciences led to the treatment of literature as just one other piece of inert matter.

In other ways, the humanists' daily practices have been affected by their concealed fondness for scientific research. However unfitting the terms, English departments talk about the writing laboratory and the reading clinic.[5] In many departments, "group dynamics" threatened for a time to be accepted as a means of developing mental acuity through rearranging the chairs. "Control group," "adequate samplings," and "standard deviation" have washed into the humanities from educational research. Teaching by machine in the laboratory is almost at hand. Taken singly, none of these works great harm. Together, they pull the humanist away from his main task of confronting the accumulated art and wisdom of mankind with an art and wisdom of his own.

The undergraduate college has suffered most from having research as a single standard of academic virtue. Under the universities' system of values, the compulsion to do research has compromised the desire to teach. Few universities consider seriously whether the two are complementary activities. Cardinal Newman believed they weren't. "To discover and teach are distinct functions," he wrote; "they are also distinct gifts, and are not commonly found united in the same persons." [6] What may be true of individual gifts is observably true of university practices. Only in the physical sciences and at an advanced level do discovery and teaching come close to being one. Everywhere else, teaching and research do not move freely along side by side but constantly rub against each other. It is not impossible for an active research scholar to be an active undergraduate teacher, but it is unlikely. The more successful he becomes, the more his research becomes the central fact of his life and the more the university frees him from teaching to permit it.

Teaching is as central to undergraduate study as research is to graduate work. The teacher of undergraduate students does not teach well by merely forcing graduate research activities into the undergraduate program. It is alarming, for example, to see the scholarly monograph becoming widely adopted texts in freshman English courses. *The King Lear Perplex* and *Huckleberry Finn: Text, Sources and Criticism,* to cite two of dozens of research source books now on the market, are as disturbing in their way as *How to Study and Take Exams.* If the scholar is not skeptical of the dubious relationship between such books and the aims of a liberal education, he might at least be suspicious of the obvious relationship between such books and the publishers' need to make money.

The undergraduate college devotes itself to awakening interests, disciplining skills, broadening the range of learning, and fostering a sense of values for the majority of students whose formal education ends with a bachelor's degree. It also provides the fundamental training and the stimulation for those who go on to advanced study. Both science and the humanities recognize these obligations. In the scientific subjects, teaching and research can be somewhat reconciled. Research in the laboratories, in the person of the research scholar, in the discoveries being made, affords awakening and discipline both for future scientists and for students with quite different aims. The university's insistence upon the humanities is insistence upon breadth and upon the consideration of values. Teaching directed toward these ends is not ordinarily served by the isolation of fact, the control of conditions, and the narrowing of focus characteristic of laboratory science.

Teaching is as close to being the humanities as research is to being science. The essential difference between the two is that teaching at the moment of doing it is a shared activity of the mind; research is not. All the humanist's yearning for the prestige of science and his chasing after its methods will not change that. Wisdom comes late in the study of the humanities; the distance between amateur interest and professional preoccupation is greater than in the sciences. A humanism subservient to research may kill a respect for humanism at the point it should engender it, at the point of confrontation between teacher and student.

I close this discussion with an example of the effects of the university's orientation toward research upon a humanistic discipline: the study of foreign languages. Even among the humanists, familiarity with and regular use of a foreign language, even through reading, is somewhat rare. In the competitive atmosphere of specialized research, there is no time to read cursorily in a language which is not the language of one's specific field. Since that means English for a majority of scholars, the cultures of the rest of the world are kept inside the continents of the Language Department, whose occupants venture out only when they need some help with a tricky point of explication in a poem or story that some foreign author inexplicably wrote in English.

At all levels of education, foreign languages are taught as mere tools rather than as the vital center of humanistic studies they once were. The term *humanities* was first used to refer to those studies devoted to the restoration of classical Latin and Greek and to the values such studies implied. The term took on large meaning because of the recognition that only through mastery of a foreign language could one begin to understand another culture. The Modern Language Association, the professional society for teachers and scholars of language and literature, states the matter clearly:

> It is therefore not the "tool" value of foreign language study that matters most—although this value now has its rapidly increasing importance. It is rather, in the concept of a liberal education, the *experience* of learning a foreign language, the experience of personally

breaking the barriers of a single speech and a single culture, that is of primary importance.[7]

Such an attitude is quite beyond and even foreign to the prevailing emphasis on foreign language study in both the public schools and the universities. The current interest in language study rises out of a sense of political necessity rather than from a desire to enlarge the student's awareness of mankind by giving him insight into how another nation thinks and feels and acts.

The universities are not precisely responsible for the attitudes toward language to be found in the public schools, though as the training centers for public school teachers, their responsibility has always been large. The Modern Language Association has been making a strenuous effort to improve language study at all levels. The humanists in the universities continue to extol the value of acquiring a second or third language, but foreign languages as a subject of specialization continue to lose ground. At the beginning of the century one graduate in eight specialized in a foreign language; now only one in eighty so specializes.[8] As yet, neither the universities nor the public schools have been able to give language study the kind of vitality that might result in its being widely recognized and practiced as a humanistic discipline.

In the graduate schools, the passing of perfunctory proficiency examinations in foreign languages has become one more Ph.D. joke. Everyone recognizes that demanding foreign language proficiency in the graduate school comes much too late. The requirement of three languages has been reduced to two, and the two have become devices by which the outright lazy or stupid or recalcitrant are slowed down or weeded out. After graduate school, languages learned in haste may stick sufficiently to enable the professor to read, with the aid of a dictionary, the epigraphs to T. S. Eliot's poems. A stubborn or better prepared scholar or one who refuses to immerse himself in research may deepen his acquaintance with other languages and so with other cultures. But publishable research, except for some of the work done by teachers of a foreign language, does not often demand facility in another tongue. The pedantry of American scholarship might be less oppressive if both professors and students were able to regard foreign languages as not mere tools for research but a necessity for aspiring humanists.

These observations by no means explore the complex problem of foreign language study in America, but they suggest that universities oriented to research must include that orientation as part of the problem.

Calling attention to some of the adverse effects of research in the universities does not deny its worth or its appeal. The nagging urge to find out and the ability to do so may well be man's small margin of superiority over other species. Almost as strong has been his urge to create, or collect, or hide away something from devouring time. In time, these individual desires have become group ones, found their way into patterns of formal education and invited society to make its needs the foremost concern of the scholar. Research not only promises society the philosopher's stone, but promises the weary thinker a safe return from that basket beneath a balloon to a solid place on earth among men and things.

The college and university's fondness for research developed out of individual desires, out of the rise of science, and out of the changes taking place in the nineteenth century which challenged the relevance of liberal arts education to the needs of society. The education of a free man remains a major objective of the liberal arts college, but the American university, for at least half a century, has been concerned with training men for an increasing number of vocations, many of which require advanced study.

Science is the tie that binds research to higher education. It is obvious that the methods of science, in an age of science, will dominate. It is hardly less obvious, though not often admitted, that science owes its high position in the eyes of the university as of the public to its success in producing things. Even when scientific research is most esoteric, most intensely focused on problems far removed from ordinary understanding, it is assumed, and probably happens, that the small discovery will lead to the larger consequence. If "basic research" works with sacred truth, "applied research" deals in secular magic. In a backhand way, the sciences in the university recognize this distinction. Those in pure science show disdain, if not contempt, for the engineers who turn thought into refrigerators, but both are allied in supporting research as the one road to truth.

Few voices inside or outside the universities challenge the dominant position of science. The President's Science Advisory Committee reporting on "Scientific Progress, the Universities, and the Federal Government," believes that most Americans are in favor of more and better science. "Scientific understanding," the report begins, "is at once highly valuable in its own right and quite indispensable for the sustained progress of a modern industrial society." [9] No one at the present time is likely to argue against that statement. On the other hand, no one can convincingly argue that science inside the university or out greatly concerns itself with questions of human values which have always been central to men's lives. The humanists can and do argue that science without a vigorous humanism is as dangerous as it appears to be at the present moment. They can and do lament that the prominence of scientific research has drawn talent and support away from the humanities. But they cannot and do not criticize the analogy with science which has made research the humanist's chief preoccupation in the universities. Failing to make that criticism, they cannot reproach science with its failure to become consequentially involved with values which the humanists themselves neglect.

The humanities have the chief responsibility for making students responsive to those ideas which become the basis for a sound system of values. There is no longer an orthodoxy which will create such values for them. The orthodoxies provided by American life with its Sunday-morning Christianity, its shifting daily ethics, its preoccupation with the this and now, are no orthodoxies at all for a great civilization. The university must find its purpose somewhere between the extremes of settling upon an orthodoxy of the past or present and of consciously seeking to free students from all orthodoxies. The modern university clearly inclines toward the latter, so strongly at times that dispassionate investigation appears to be all that counts and the humanistic studies seem to be valued chiefly for their usefulness in an age of increasing leisure. The humanistic concern for values should be as impatient with indifference as with indoctrination. Stressing the importance of values does not mean forsaking intellectual growth for the inculcation of moral principles. Nor does it mean diminishing the demands for exactness, for disciplined study, for rigorous thought. It principally means the maintaining of a fairly constant sense of relationship between the thing investigated and the human existence which makes that investigation possible. More specifically, it means awakening the student's mind to engage itself not merely with isolated fact, however beguiling, but with facts set against values broadly based and intensely examined.

11. Money

COLLEGES are like the family in D. H. Lawrence's "The Rocking-Horse Winner," bedeviled by the phrase, "There must be more money." The cry, of course, is not the scholar's alone. It probably began as a demand for more clamshells or beaver pelts. Harold Clark, surveying earnings in various occupations in the thirties, concluded that "one of the most striking things revealed by the investigation was the consistency with which each occupation maintained it was underpaid." [1] What gives poignancy if not force to the academic man's plea is that he has been voicing it for so long, has so steadfastly asserted the high value of his work, and has cried out over a conscience which finds toiling for glory superior to working for pay.

Despite the hard cash realities of paying for higher education, colleges and universities persist in regarding themselves as vaguely philanthropic enterprises. The reasons are many. Underlying all are the Hebraic and Hellenic traditions which, at times, seem devoted to impoverishing those most dedicated to keeping them alive. Teaching began as a family enterprise, and as it separated itself from the family it had difficulty separating itself from family economics. The Hebraic tradition was a tribal, familial tradition in which education was not a marketable commodity but a part of sacred ritual. The Greek tradition, originally tribal and familial, later personal and intimate, and still later, social and urban, included both the Sophists and Socrates. Even the influence of Aristotle, who put money among life's "goods," did not much alter the idea that "love of wisdom" was alien to "love of money."

To look at the long traditions of higher education is to find scarcely a single time in which the scholar thought he was paid well. "Few men, nowadays," wrote Libanius, a famous teacher of the fourth century A.D., "grow rich by teaching." Libanius describes a scholar seeking his salary at Antioch in the mid-fourth century:

> Sometimes he gets only a part, sometimes none at all, sometimes it comes by driblets. And then, the bother that he is put to, to get it even so! He must go to the governor, or to the governor's attendants, or to the city treasurer, and demean himself by fawning upon his inferiors and begging for what is his own, and these are actions which, I am very sure, the man of self-respect, such as the teacher should be, would almost rather starve than do. And then, the meanness of this salary! Some call it enough, but I am ashamed to mention how small it is.[2]

At least, Libanius knew both good times and bad. The best of the Sophists during much of his lifetime earned substantial salaries; some became wealthy men.

The academic traditions in the Renaissance were not only Hebraic and Hellenic but Christian as well. All favored keeping the scholar poor. Before the decline of the Empire, some Roman courts refused to grant judgments to teachers trying to collect student fees by ruling that the occupation of a philosopher was inconsistent with a demand for money. The monastic tradition found the teacher's financial demands not only legally but morally indefensible. Higher education through most of its early existence was supported by charitable giving of one kind or another. The early European universities exacted more direct support from students, but patronage, from individuals or the state, remained the chief source of funds. Universities with generous patronage prospered; the majority consoled themselves with the superior riches of the spirit.

In the American colonies, higher learning led a marginal existence almost everywhere through the seventeenth and eighteenth centuries. The economy could with difficulty support an academic profession, and both the college and the church were strongly dependent upon charity. The alliance between piety, poverty, and the higher learning was a part of the history of most colleges and universities founded in the nineteenth century. The twentieth century differs only in that the secularization of higher learning has brought with it an uncharitable recognition of the need for money. Judging from the repeated cries of insolvency coming from the colleges and universities during the past fifty years, one can only conclude that recognition has not yet led to sure ways of getting it. Even in the golden years of American philanthropy when John D. Rockefeller was starting the University of Chicago with a grant of $2,000,000 and Leland Stanford was debating, so the story goes, whether to establish a new college or to buy Harvard, the chorus of complaint about salaries, the gloom over being able to keep institutions alive, was depressingly like the lamentation of our own time.

The basic difficulties of university financing are related to the need for large sums of money taken from large numbers of people to support a central enterprise which pays no direct dividends, depletes the family and the community, and demands at least four years of partial or total idleness from American youth. Such wanton economic acts are not designed to encourage investment or to attract support. Educational and general expenses for higher education now comprise about .80 per cent of the gross national product, about half the amount spent on cigarettes.[3] But "cigarettes taste good like cigarettes should"; they get bought for 30 cents a pack and consumed shortly after with a brief but immediate satisfaction. Paying for a college education is a different matter. The product is high-priced, the payments cannot be deferred, satisfactions are delayed, fitful, and often unrelated to the act of consumption. In the face of these realities, the money coming into higher education is never going to come easily and never going to be enough.

For the individual, the cost of college education is likely to become increasingly burdensome, not beyond the ability of reasonably foresighted parents and reasonably energetic individuals to provide, though somewhat beyond their willingness to pay. The bills are large, not so much for tuition as for keeping the student alive and happy. Expenses for tuition, books, and fees range from as little as $150 a year in a state university to over $1500 a year in an Ivy League school. Board and room charges range from about $600 to $1200 a year. At one of the prominent state universities the total of these expenses might approach $1000 a year; at one of the top private schools, $3000. These are minimum figures. Attendant expenses—clothes, parties, autos, train and plane fare, memberships, and the rest—are proportional to the prestige (and the cost) of the college. The high life, however, is offered at many colleges, and may cost as much in Madison, Wisconsin, as in New Haven, Connecticut. A survey of actual spending by individual students in 1957 showed total expenses ranging from $200 a year to $5500.[4]

For many reasons, and whatever the cost, individuals are reluctant to pay. College expenses come at the wrong time. Parents have been looking forward to the day the children are grown, awaiting the fulfillment of personal desires long deferred or simply awaiting an end to the considerable expenses of raising a family. The expectation of seeing either a boy or girl become self-supporting at eighteen dwindles year by year, just as the expectation of further schooling rises. Above all, for most families, college expenses are the first educational expenses which must be met out of pocket. A Roper survey in 1959 disclosed that two-thirds of the nation's parents expected their children to attend college but few had done anything about it. Sixty per cent had no savings plans. The others were putting away approximately $150 a year. The attitude of most seemed to be based on that fundamental economic premise that someone, somewhere, at some time, would provide. Many were like the woman who could hardly wait until the day she could send her children away to college to keep them from eating her out of house and home.

Not only the individual's tenacious grasp of the dollar, but the public's response to the over-all costs of higher education, make college financing difficult. Higher education outside the sports pages appears chiefly in stories about students' misbehavior, professors' eccentricities, and legislative appropriations. In my state, Utah, the appropriation for higher education this biennium was $31,000,000, a large sum in the minds of local taxpayers. Utah's expenditure for higher education is 18 per cent of its state tax revenue, a higher percentage than that of any other state. At the other extreme, New York and Massachusetts spend approximately 2.5 per cent.[5] However, in these states, the number of expensive private schools is proportionately large. Fund drives like Harvard's for $82,000,000 or Columbia's for $68,000,000 remind the citizens of the size of higher education's needs. Million-dollar amounts are still awesome, and no one but schoolboys or national defense experts talks knowledgeably about billions. The public, strongly affected by memories of preinflation prices, is bound to find current spending for higher education a source of apprehension.

Colleges and universities, formerly numbered among society's luxuries which could be purchased in good times and foregone in bad, are now big businesses demanding increasing support at all times. There is no question that the affluent society can support a much-expanded, much-improved system of higher education, nor is there much of a question that more money needs to be spent in this vital area of private and public interest. The growth of higher education, the expense of individual institutions, and the dwindling of great private fortunes have moved the support of higher education far beyond what private philanthropy can provide. State and municipal appropriations, endowments and investments, voluntary contributions from individuals and organizations have carried the burden of support of American higher education. In the future, colleges and universities must look to the individual citizen for more support, both in increased tax revenues and increased tuition income from students and their parents.

Faculty salaries are the central economic fact of university existence, not only because they comprise the biggest single item in a university's operating budget, but because the quality of the faculty determines the quality of the school. In an average budget, instructional costs are probably about one-third of the total, a fact that confirms the feeling that instruction is not the American university's all-consuming concern. For the faculty, salaries are always too small. There is a monotonous sameness in the cry for higher salaries from 1900 to the present. A report on the financial status of the profession prepared by the Carnegie Foundation in 1908 observed:

> . . . While college salaries can never be made the equal of those paid in large business enterprises, it is clearly to the interest not only of the professor himself, but of the students and of society in general, that his salary should in all places approach the line of comfort. That it does not do so in most American colleges is only too clearly proved by the statistics given in this bulletin.[6]

The conclusion to an AAUP Committee Report on the same subject in 1956 is not very different:

> It is clear that the profession has retrogressed so much in economic status over the past sixteen years that, as things stand, its capacity to maintain and renew itself may be gravely weakened.[7]

Since 1956, the increased competition for men and women with advanced degrees has forced salaries somewhat higher. Professors are not as poor as they seemed in 1956, nor are their cries of anguish as loud. Nevertheless, when the academic man compares his salary with other professional salaries, he can hardly escape feeling that he is underpaid. In 1959, Department of Commerce figures showed the following average salaries for professional employment in federal government: engineering, $9204; legal services, $9725; fine and applied arts, $8897; and education $6400. The average salary for faculty in undergraduate colleges was $6810.[8]

As a member of a profession, the college teacher possesses specialized skills beyond the reach of the majority of men; only medicine requires a longer period of schooling. Above all, the college professor is responsible for producing college graduates. The predicted average starting pay for the class of 1961 was $5640 for men and slightly less for women, just about what a beginning college instructor could expect after having completed from two to seven more years of schooling.

Average salary figures in the academic profession are somewhat misleading, for salaries tend to vary as widely as institutions. At the low end, the need for higher salaries is not based upon claims of worth or skill or length of training so much as upon the gap between income and expenditure, between the kind of life the professor can lead and the kind society has led him to expect. But this argument has more strength of sentiment than economic force. Pity for the economic plight of those who stay within Limbo has to be tempered by considering the many reasons which make impoverishment a voluntary choice. At the upper end, salaries afford a degree of comfort which helps keep the desire to have more from overcoming the aversion to go about getting it. The weakness of the profession at the bottom and the comparative comfort at the top throws the responsibility upon the middle range of schools for moving the profession to a better economic position.

Despite economic realities, many academic men still find an interest in money a kind of self-seeking at odds with their academic ideals. Even now, the shortage of faculty is being regarded as much an educational crisis as an economic opportunity. Idealistic sentiments are heightened by a fondness for security and prestige. Though professors insist upon free enterprise and laissez faire in scholarship, they drift toward equalitarianism and protectionism in salaries. At the time when private enterprise was most fiercely competitive, the academic profession was most contemptuous of such vulgar practices. The profession is getting a harder heart, but it still not only tolerates weaknesses but protects them. Tenure, for all its blessings, sacrifices income, not precisely for the freedom to be a scholar, but for freedom to be an idle one. On many university faculties, the deadwood is considerable, identifiable—and invulnerable. Faculties accept the risks of indulging the inept and the lazy in return for the security of stable though small incomes spread somewhat equally throughout the institution. It is not that faculty members would not like to have higher incomes; it is that they will accept lower ones if the alternative is to turn to the competitive economics which prevail outside. Faculty members also pay something for the dignity of maintaining the four academic ranks. Financial progress from instructor to full professor is often a slow procession through small space. Colleges long on prestige but short on salary are competing for faculty with bustling institutions which send out salary schedules charting the increases from Steps One through

Eighteen. Conditions of teaching are often less attractive at such aggressive institutions, but the faculty member who resists an offer is in part keeping respectability at the price of a lower wage.

Thus the academic man asserts his superiority to the vulgar pursuit of money. The world outside replies by regarding the professor's work as effete, easily performed, and of dubious utility. Bluntly, it thinks the professor is worth about what he gets; if he tried to compete in the world outside, he couldn't make as much. Such an attitude is based upon an antiquated idea of college life as foreign to the fact as is the belief that academic men are still gentlemen and scholars. For many reasons, the genteel life at the university has passed away. The ivory towers have been razed for parking lots. Not only are there more students to be taught, to be chaperoned, to be recorded, but more books and articles and instruments to be read and written and kept abreast of. There are more committees and institutes and projects within the university and more lectureships, research grants, and assignments in the world outside.

The growing worldliness of the modern university has not increased the public's willingness to entrust professors with large sums of money. It has, however, afforded a delusively attractive way of meeting the faculty's desire for more money without paying higher salaries. The university pays its faculty the salaries it can afford; the world at large makes up the rest for specific services. This has meant a little more money for all, much more money for the academic promoters and freebooters. Unfortunately, it is a bad way. Having a faculty earn a sizable portion of its income for outside work strengthens the inclination of the public to regard academic teaching and scholarship as no work at all; it provides one more excuse for inadequate support; it consumes a faculty's resources which should be spent on contemplation and the acquiring of wisdom; it furthers the tendency within the profession to lack high and firm standards. Some faculty members prefer, on high grounds of professional integrity, to avoid all manner of extra income; others do all manner of tasks. Some, longing to serve, have no opportunity. Others take opportunities which cut them off from future professional development. Pushed to an extreme, academic moonlighting would turn the universities into an economic chance world in which avowed professional standards would be as distant from actual practices as announced salaries from actual income. Virtue alone —which academic men have long regarded as their particular form of wealth—may keep them from becoming merely acquisitive.

Faculties are being neither greedy nor vain in insisting that college teaching should have a high professional status and the financial position to support it. University training is at the heart of an affluent, complex, highly specialized, and tremendously productive society which demands the expanding of knowledge, the development of skills, and the bringing about of an ever more informed citizenry. The judgments citizens make as to the relative values of different occupations do much to determine the character and the well-being of the society. Since higher education is so closely tied to direct public support, what, in general, the college teacher receives for his services reflects rather directly the valuation placed upon higher education. To maintain a vital profession's ability to function well—and to function for the good of the whole society—that profession must have the kind of professional status which the public will respect, honor, and seek to perpetuate.

Academic men not only have economic wants common to all men in a prosperous society but other particular wants related to their profession. A teacher needs to participate in and stimulate intellectual life. He should be able to broaden his outlook and in turn those of his students—by travel, by study at home and abroad, by participation in the life outside the university. He should be able to contribute his share of support to community activities—to symphonies, libraries, voters' groups, charities, scholarship funds. If his position provides for nine months of classroom work and three months for professional development, the salary should be such as to make that development possible. Most of all, a college teacher's salary should enable him to keep his mind above the everlasting picking after corn which has turned public school intellectual life largely into a contemplation of the schoolteacher's abused condition. A profession which cannot maintain its self-respect cannot hope to attract the number and kind of teachers needed in the years ahead.

Faculty members like to oppose their transient flesh to the enduring stone of university buildings. They generally assume that a university president has an edifice complex or a mortar fixation, with as much regard for the pun as for the truth. Both the presidents and the public like the appearance of an impressive campus, but buildings are going up today at about the same slow rate as faculty salaries. The faculty may spend as much time complaining about the places in which they work as in lamenting their pay.

Colleges are both victims and beneficiaries of traditions. The Gothic quadrangle and the garden campus are attractive but expensive places of learning. The truly economical university would probably be a single building somewhat like the Pentagon, ringed with parking lots, vibrant with electronic devices, paced by the moving belt and the ringing bell, and filled with students and faculty twenty-four hours a day. Cost, however, is but one consideration and not necessarily the most important one. The quadrangle and the garden campus are based on sound theory, and modern life has, if anything, given greater point to it. The contemplative life requires some shutting out of the world, whether by closing a heavy oak door or by passing through the campus gates. Four years is little enough time for the young reared in the hodgepodge of the cities, the sprawling sameness of the suburbs, or the gas-station rural of the small towns to find himself in surroundings which invite contemplation. At a time when natural beauty—where it still exists—attracts the developer more than the artist, the enclosed campus is its own excuse for being, whatever its cost. The green expanses, handsome landscaping, and unified architecture of a college campus answer to man's need to place his activities in a concordant setting. Located in urban centers, the campus reveals man's relation to nature; in a rural landscape, it adds a civilizing presence. The point is often passed over in the struggle for money, and state legislatures and private donors are to be congratulated for being sufficiently responsive to these values in the past to make campuses as handsome as many of them are.[9]

In the decade ahead, the increased costs of acquiring land and of erecting buildings will make it difficult to maintain space and greensward and harmony. Many campuses have already been marred by the practice of putting permanent buildings on every available open spot, of plowing under the grass for parking lots, of accepting motel modern as the prevailing style, and of planning without regard for quiet or comfort. University building and planning are always well intentioned, but they are greatly at the mercy of financial necessity and the values prevailing on and off campus. New fieldhouses get built and old administration buildings expensively maintained as a kind of compromise between appeasing the public's desires and honoring the academic tradition. Other campus buildings, having no such compelling arguments for their construction, do not get built or get built badly.

The relationships between setting and living, between buildings and learning, between those who occupy them and what goes on in them, needs more attention than it ordinarily gets. Shelters cannot be designed to fit the shape of thought, but that general idea needs to be implanted in the architect's mind. In general, campus building is characterized by inflexibility and small insight. In the classroom buildings, provisions for small rooms, large rooms, and middle-sized rooms are about the extent of tailoring to fit the needs of instruction. For dormitories, the prevailing model is the Hilton Hotel. In all buildings, architectural success is most evident in the plumbing; whatever new campus buildings lack, there are certain to be adequate toilets with separate facilities for men, women, and faculty.

The architect's intentions seldom reflect an awareness of academic life, and original plans are often changed because of the need for economy. One of the newest buildings on my campus is of the conventional skin and glass construction, with the longest expanse facing a burning western sun. The plans called for air-conditioning, but air-conditioning was not provided for in the legislative appropriation. As was expected, many of the rooms proved unbearable for half the day from April to December, and air conditioning was later installed at greater expense and at the sacrifice of two offices. In the same building, faculty office space was originally planned as a collection of cubicles partitioned off by dividers rising to half the room's height. The architect's idea was to use these for brief consultations between students and faculty and to provide ruminating quarters for the faculty in a separate building. Here the legislative committee's eye to economy proved superior to the architect's design. Separate offices were provided in the classroom building, and the faculty was spared explicit identification with the finance company.

The building programs now in evidence on most campuses still run well behind present needs and far behind anticipated needs. More students mean more buildings or more extensive use of buildings. The administrators talk about the latter as "full plant utilization," and treat it as the first of many economies which would put money in the professor's pocket and new carpet in the president's office. To the efficiency-minded, the fact that classroom buildings sit idle a part of the day seems to be shock-ingly wasteful. To others, like Lee DuBridge, president of Cal. Tech., a university's worth, or even its efficiency, cannot be measured by how many hours each foot of space is occupied. "Why do we use the bedroom in our houses only 6 to 8 hours a day?" he wrote. "Why not take turns sleeping and make one bedroom do the work of three?"[10] The point is well taken, though its truth has another side. Bedrooms do receive a minimum use of eight hours a day; if a college classroom could come up to that, the plant utilizers might be satisfied.

Universities are probably not yet ready to give in to the demand for efficiency. Economy is not a subject the faculty likes. It most often appears as an administrative move to make conditions as unpleasant as possible while keeping salaries as low as ever. I have already argued the merits of the kind of campus which is not "efficient," which is not only costly to build but costly to maintain. The academic man may be willing to trade part of his salary for a pleasant classroom or a comfortable place to study or a few hundred feet of campus lawn. Necessity may force him to look for economies, but he will continue to support practices which are uneconomical but defended by academic traditions and his own habits.

Consider the matter of morning classes. If it were not for the laboratory sciences, athletics, and the graduate schools, college instruction would fall pretty much between the hours of 8 and 12. The economic advantages of making the afternoon hours as full as the morning ones are obvious. The arguments against it are defenses of a way of life rather than reasoned support of specific practices. Going to school in the morning and playing in the afternoon is appealing, but is it a fundamental rhythm of life? If morning hours are the prime time for learning, the student might be better employed in the library than in the classroom. A ministry of fun can operate as well in the morning as in the afternoon. Nor does the need for part-time employment seem consequential. Employers, already in the universities' debt for a supply of cheap and reasonably bright labor, can make use of it at one time as well as another. Colleges and universities could run classes throughout the day whenever they wished to exercise a firm hand. The chief obstacles are not the desires of the student but the inflexible ways of the university.

Or take class size and the ratio of students to faculty as another example. Both of these are central to Beardsley Ruml's and Donald Morrison's *Memo to a College Trustee.* The book shows clearly that a liberal arts college willing to raise the ratio of students to faculty and to reconsider the desire for uniformly small classes could make substantial savings in operating costs. I have not heard faculty members speak highly of the book, even though it proposes doubling their salaries. There is, I suspect, a justified suspicion that quality will be sacrificed in the adoption of a plan that has as its center the simple expedient of having more students and fewer faculty. At the same time, the proposal arouses faculty resistance because of the reflections it casts upon entrenched faculty habits. Is a faculty member ready to have his favorite courses examined in terms of his university's or even his own financial needs? Is he willing to consider whether the lecturing he is fond of is the best way to deal with his subject? Is he willing to give up his free time in the afternoon for a sounder plan of operation? Is he willing to face financial facts related to curriculum and teaching practices which may lead to embarrassing questions about his own activities?

In many ways, ingrained habits keep the university from getting more from both buildings and dollars. Savings are open to any university willing to hack away at courses and credits: course programs instead of credit hours; yearly registration instead of quarter by quarter; fewer but more meaningful incentives instead of grades. Simply diminishing the number of classes and lecture hours required of students and increasing the demand for independent study would save both space and money. In the rapidly expanding nonresidential colleges, paperbacks and the family bedroom provide the necessaries for study off campus; in residential colleges, dormitories which encourage learning outside the classroom are the only kind worth maintaining. Checking the university's inordinate desire continually to expand services and to minister to the students' welfare would cut down on expenditures of many kinds. Finally, the bureaucracy, described in a previous chapter, devours money as it breeds machines.

The basic facts about money for higher education are clear. Costs are going up; faculties will demand and get more; buildings will have to be built; economies will be hard to achieve. Colleges are like individuals. They, too, like someone else to foot the bills—not the students or the faculty for they are the college, but the state, or the donor, or the endowment fund. Unfortunately, sources which could be relied on in the past are less capable of meeting expenses today. As a result, some or all of these developments may be expected in the next decade.[11]

In both public and private institutions, income is likely to be derived more equally from the various sources of funds. At present, some sources bear a disproportionate share of the expense. In public institutions, funds from state, local, and national governments comprise about 60 per cent of income. In private institutions, tuition is the largest single source, about 33 per cent of the total. Endowments, gifts, and grants are a small portion of income for public universities, about 3 per cent. In private ones, they amount to 20 per cent. These figures are for higher education as a whole; the distribution of support varies widely with each college or university. In the years ahead, the distinction between private and public institutions in terms of support will become less marked. Tuition will certainly become a more important source of income in public institutions, just as government support in the form of research contracts, loans and students aid will become more important in private ones. In public institutions, gifts and grants, particularly those coming from alumni fund drives, will become larger, and in both the contributions of business may be expected to increase. The advantages of widening the base of support, of making both public and private institutions less dependent upon one major source of income, of bringing public and private institutions more closely together, seem worth the risk involved in lessening the duality of higher education.

The argument between those who advocate low or no tuition in public colleges and universities and those who feel that tuition should be increased to pay a higher portion of the cost will be hotly waged during the next decade.[12] With the increasing expenditures of state governments, their reluctance to increase tax support for higher education, and the rising level of personal income, tuition increases in the public institutions seem unavoidable. To me, such increases seem both logical and just. Neither the argument from the tradition of low tuitions nor the loose democratic argument resting upon the state's responsibility to provide free public education at all levels is convincing. The difficulties state universities are undergoing now in trying to admit every applicant suggest that twelve years of indifferent performance and limited demonstration of capacity do not justify four more. The democratic strength of higher education as a whole can not be increased by the weakening of private institutions which often goes with their attempts to compete with low-tuition universities. Higher tuition, accompanied as it must be, by a much expanded program of scholarships, could help keep both the public and private universities strong and the doors wide open to all those who could profit from further education. In addition, higher tuition would have a not inconsiderable advantage of confronting the public with the fact that a good advanced education cannot be cheap, and that someone has to pay. Since most financially sound private schools have already raised tuitions to more nearly approximate costs, public institutions might move to establish a reasonable ratio between their tuitions and those of comparable private schools. A tuition half that of the comparable private institution might not be too high.

Federal support of higher education is almost certain to increase.[13] The federal government is already heavily involved in higher education, chiefly through grants and contracts for research, but also through grants to land-grant colleges, various student aid programs, disposal of land and surplus property, and loans for buildings. In 1957–1958, the federal government provided $535 million of the $1,752 million which came from all government sources. The debate over federal aid is a question of what kind and how much. The universities, as well as the public, have an important stake in seeing that federal support is soundly planned and administered. The large amounts the government currently invests in research grants and contracts is not federal aid, but payment for services the government desires. These expenses have been the major item added to the modern university's budget, and the government has paid only part of the cost. More direct federal aid, of the kind proposed in last year's education bill, traps a large part of the public in a number of paradoxes. In many states, the state legislators most reluctant to provide funds for state universities are the ones most set against federal aid. Similarly, those states which most need federal aid are often those whose citizens bark most fiercely about states' rights and the individual's ability to take care of himself.

Finally, the business community, many of which are opposed to federal aid, is not yet contributing what it could and what its dependence upon higher education should lead it to contribute.[14] Corporation giving has greatly increased, from $40 million in 1950 to about $100 million in 1956, and to an estimated $170 million in 1960. It now provides about 17 per cent of private contributions to higher education. That amount, according to the Council for Financial Aid to Education, is not enough; it estimates a need for $600 million each year from philanthropic and corporate giving. As Seymour Harris points out, with a maximum tax allowance of 5 per cent of income, tax-free contributions from corporations to the extent of 2 per cent would yield almost $1 billion today, $1.5 billion or more ten years from now. (He also points out that such giving is an excellent way of exacting government contributions without danger of interference.) An editorial in a Salt Lake City newspaper, commenting on figures similar to those given above, drew its conclusion succinctly: "The challenge to industry and business is clear enough; either they will meet it or the federal government will move ever more deeply into the field, with ever higher taxes to pay the bill." [15] As the corporation has replaced the individual as the chief possessor of large sums of money, it needs to take on the philanthropic spirit through which private capital once went into higher education. In those days, university presidents used to hover at the bedside. How to move the heart of the corporation is an equal challenge today.

12. The Persistence of Problems

PEOPLE, ideas, and money, and the problems they create, are the eternal verities around which university committees, self-study groups, and policy-making bodies perpetually cluster. That their deliberations come to so little testifies to the durability of truth as to the vanity of academic endeavors. Abraham Flexner, writing about the American universities in 1930, called the changes since the opening of Johns Hopkins in 1876 "amazing, immensely to the credit of a people that within a few generations has had to subdue a continent, create a social and political order, maintain its unity, and invent educational, philanthropic, sanitary, and other agencies capable of functioning at all." [1] No such changes have taken place in the past thirty years. The criticisms which are the focus of Dr. Flexner's book—that the American universities have "needlessly cheapened, vulgarized and mechanized themselves"—are as applicable today, though perhaps not to the same universities, as they were then.

The need is still for university education that is serious and responsible, concerned with idea, not mere fact, with the spirit of man as well as his possessions, with the larger issues of human existence rather than with daily practicalities. The abuses discussed in the previous section have neither abated nor disappeared. The difficulties of finding financial support for our greatly expanded system of higher education are no less today than in the past, and the possibilities of overcoming them are no more encouraging. The developments within the American university during the past thirty years serve only to confirm that university problems, large and small, have tenacious and enduring lives.

The teasing question is "Why?" What is there about the academic mind and the university body that causes so few problems to be solved and keeps so many eternally poised for solution? It is easy for a simple mind to assume that problems exist merely to be solved. The academic mind is more subtle; problem-solving and brain-storming are functions assigned to the simpler parts of the organism—colleges of education or schools of social work, for example. The higher faculties are happier with continuation than with conclusion, with compromise than with conviction. University thought falls naturally into the Socratic method, but having neither so sharp nor directing a dialectic as Socrates's, it tends toward endless debate. It is happiest not when it has reached a firm conclusion but when it has discovered that the arguments are so precisely balanced that no conclusion is possible. Only a faculty group could find satisfaction in such a report as this:

> While the report showed a majority of the schools studied were on a semester basis, the study recognized that both semester systems and quarter systems differ widely among themselves; also that while the quarter system imposes the greatest costs for the registrar's office, it was felt that the possibility of registering for a full year should be explored. In general, it was believed that there was no advantage with either system, that different results might be obtained, depending on how you work.[2]

Even for a university document, the prose in this report has a high density, but the substance is representative of the end of most academic deliberations. "Μέν" and "δέ"—"on the one hand," and "on the other"—an eminent classical scholar pointed out, helped shape the Greek way of thought.[3] The academic man has not only these, but "perhaps" and its euphemisms: "seems," "appears," "indicates," "suggests," and such compounded evasions as "perhaps it may be likely to appear," or "it seems scarcely unlikely that" or "perhaps a tentative hypothesis which might be here hinted at."

Caution, humility, and tentativeness have their worth, but they can be praised overmuch. Respected too highly, they become excuses not to think rather than restraints upon looseness and conceit. The fondness for qualification which smothers academic prose exposes an uneasiness toward the value of the search as well as toward its complexities. The French, of all peoples the most aware of the traits of academicians, have the proverbs that describe the workings of the academic mind. *Tout lasse, tout casse, tout passe* is one; *tout comprendre, c'est tout pardonner* is the other.

The university personality has an unusually high level of tolerance for human weaknesses. The undergraduate folklore about irascible professors grows up not because of the curmudgeon's ubiquity, but because even a polite sorehead stands out in the company of placid gentlemen. University professors are an amiable lot, even though that amiability may not break out in Rotarian back-slapping. A folksy humanism pervades the campus, making policy flexible and regulations easily bent. A student transgressor can always find some faculty member to plead his case, and faculty members are notorious for their own small evasions, like ignoring library notices and parking fines, and for larger ones, like relaxing the rules for promotion and tenure. Such flexibility may be necessary for survival in the entangled bureaucracy where the foe one faces may be one's better self, but it doesn't develop an academic habit of facing either human or institutional failings squarely.

The life of reason, of moderation, of judgment may not call forth courage, decision, and action as quickly as lives lived closer to passion and physical violence. The nature of academic life may attract men of a somewhat phlegmatic temperament. In the arts and letters, for example, such men probably prefer the security of an academic life to the alternative of confronting society with nothing but a raw, creative talent which hopes to produce what the public will buy. However exhausting the Ph.D. program may be, it has the great advantage of prescribing a path, which, if followed, will lead to a yearly contract at a modest salary with some rewards for ambition and some room for individual initiative. In the sciences, it should be said, individuals may find university scholarship and teaching more a matter of first choice than of an unwillingness to accept the alternatives. The universities are now *the* centers for research, and no good case can be made that the universities chiefly attract those scientists who find pursuing their special interest too difficult in the world outside. Nevertheless, the very skill that first-rate scientists possess and the demands which their research makes upon them may limit their active involvement in the ongoing life of the university.

My observations may seem to support the familiar academic stereotype. "In America," George Cram Cook wrote in 1913, "there are three sexes—men, women, and professors." [4] Claude Bowman's informative survey of the college professor as he appeared in the general magazines from 1890 to 1938 shows that the image of ineffectuality was widely accepted by individuals inside and outside the profession. The stereotype contains about as little truth—and as much—as most stereotypes. The academic personality is not all one set of characteristics, but among the prominent traits are caution, reserve, a strong need for security, a reluctance to venture, and liberalism toward society at a distance, conservatism toward society close at hand.

These natural predispositions are strengthened by academic experience. One of the saddest and yet inescapable facts of institutional life is that young tigers become middle-aged house cats. Chart the course of any man's acquaintance with an institution. The less he knows of it, the more he criticizes it. Put him into daily, intimate relationship with its workings and the criticisms soften. What appeared stupid turns out to be passably wise under the circumstances; what appeared unfair proves to be judicious in respect to the conflicting interests involved; what appeared intolerable shows itself to be a complex problem with which the best minds and hearts in the institution are struggling.

In the universities, this means that any man over forty or with over five years' service is institutional as well as individual. The old guard is a recognizable part of every college or university; what often escapes notice is that its members need not be very old or have very much to guard. In universities not marked by excessive inbreeding, the presence of outsiders helps temper the self-esteem of the locals and keeps the institution from becoming overpoweringly smug. The outsider is able to see with eyes unaffected by sentiment or made unobservant by a continuing familiarity. The time it takes for an outsider to become localized is about the time that he remains useful as a critic and as a force for reform. Few men desire to remain permanent transients or relish being continually identified with every cause. Sooner or later, almost all members of an academic community, outsiders or locals, take on the characteristics of the institution.

The organization of the university, with its complex balancing of powers, strongly inclines the course of the university to a middle path. The division into colleges, the colleges into departments, the departments into numerous specialized provinces, defy all efforts to fix upon a central purpose. The many contending forces—trustees, alumni, students, and the public—pull the university this way and that. Major changes have usually been accomplished by a strong president whose will, however opposed by the other forces, is single and can be applied rapidly and with vigor. Few faculties have been able to act in a similar way, and, in fact, in their insistence upon democratic government, often stand in opposition to the executive will. Legislators suspicious of left-wing professors need only immerse themselves in university politics to gain assurance that academic men are fiercely, if oftentimes ineffectively, democratic. They would find, too, that this insistence upon democracy increases as an institution becomes more intellectual. They might even gain insight into democracy's basic weaknesses; like other democracies, universities are ponderous, slow to act, and betrayed by the apathy of their citizens.

Despite the high intelligence and the limited number of citizens of even a large university, faculty senates, compromised by conflicting self-interests, restricted to formal patterns of procedure, and plagued by the divided attentions of their members, are more debating societies than effective formulators of policy. Their deliberations hover around dead center where every proposal is tabled or under committee study. Nothing is quite as revealing in an unintended way as the institutional self-studies so popular in the past decade. These are usually financed by foundations, prepared by committees, pickled in standard university prose, and stored in libraries throughout the land. Their accomplishments speak faintly through the verbiage, as in the following excerpts from a year-long study in which I once participated:

> A valuable result has been substantial progress toward the adoption of a more effective program. . . . Possibly more important still have been the intangible benefits of the stimulation and reinvigoration of the thinking of the entire faculty through its full participation in the study. . . . Clearer perspective and increased objectivity in individual approach to educational problems have been stimulated, and temptations toward educational dogmatism have been largely overcome, as the complexity and ramifications of problems became apparent in the process of the meetings of minds of colleagues striving to resolve conflicting considerations.[5]

University self-studies, like university work of any kind, depend heavily upon committees. Though a good part of the university has learned and practices the cruel lesson that study is a lonely occupation, the university studies itself only in groups. Perhaps this is because such self-study is regarded as secondary work, or busy work, or downright distasteful work—so much so that it is easier borne in groups. Or it may reflect the general attractiveness of group study to many lonely scholars who at times seem huddled around round tables for the creation of committee assignments for all. Whatever it is, the committee is often a clotting agent in the circulation of ideas.

The committee is a way of granting faculties a voice in university government with a fair chance of their never using it effectively. Similarly, faculty senates and councils are weakened by the basic rule that in politics as in tennis, the advantage rests with the server. The power of administration is down from a point of firm control; it not only initiates many measures but presides over the discussions. The power of a faculty is up from chaos. The relative strength of each can be deduced from these positions. The faculty is prolific of individual grievances; it is barren in getting these grievances into the form of legislation. Legislation is often achieved by exhaustion, faculty members wearily passing measures and withdrawing opposition after the prime hours have been consumed in a tedious march through the agenda. Even when legislation is enacted it is, like much congressional legislation, deformed by the amendments necessary to its being enacted. Like other legislative bodies, faculty groups work with sharp awareness of what can be put into practice. Since, at the level of action, control is given to the department and to committees within the department and even to individual faculty members who teach the classes, the ideal legislation is that which will affect no one very greatly. The most frustrating act of university life is to consider the many casual ideas afloat for improving the quality of the university and the few that ever find their way into university policies and practices.

The academic personality and the organization of the universities conspire together to keep the university on even keel—and aground. As if these were not sufficient, a number of other peculiarities of university existence work to the same end.

The shape of the year, for example, surely has something to do with the way in which the academic engine builds up a head of steam by spring only to have it leak away during the summer. Spring is the cruelest time in academia. Then, if ever, academic life has accumulated enough energy to give the impression that it is going somewhere. Summer vacation saves it the trip. Academic men, being perpetual schoolboys, go through life anticipating the time when they can get rid of satchel and books and get away. It may be, of course, only to different books and a different set of papers in the satchel, but the illusion is as important as the reality. Faculty meetings in the spring are almost as silly as faculty meetings in the fall. In the spring, the committees report. The chairmen hand out the mimeographed reports, then read them, item by item, comma by comma. The president reviews a successful year; a few faculty members doze; the business vice president explains why buildings are going up and the faculty salaries aren't; more faculty members doze; the academic vice president explains that academic freedom has never been more glorious, teaching more vigorous, prospects more pleasing; the rest of the faculty doze. Supposedly, matters of continuing consequence to the university are going on while administrators talk and faculty members doze. But next fall's faculty meetings begin at the beginning all over again, as if no committees had ever met, no reports ever been given, no heights ever reached, no prospects ever described.

Higher education is formal education, and breaking away from the patterns which tradition imposes is difficult. The nine-month year hangs on from its reasonable adoption in an agricultural society to its becoming an archaism in an industrial one. Any close scrutiny of the practice, however, reveals that unsuspected virtues lurk there. Summers are hot and air conditioning expensive. Vacation habits still favor the summer months. Athletic competition depends on the three seasons, as do fall mixers and winter carnivals and spring proms. Thus, the obvious wisdom of using the full year is overruled by accumulated arguments based upon habit and tradition.

Once listed in the official Calendar of Events, every act in which more than two people engage at more than random intervals becomes a tradition. The more years they are tolerated, the more they argue their intrinsic worth. Football, even at its most corrupt, gives students an emotional center of identity. The academic procession and the wearing of cap and gown arouse a sense of value beyond the contemplation of profits being made by academic costumers. Greek letter societies maintained in the universities ensure that the classical alphabet shall not soon disappear from the earth. By now, it must be obvious that even the reading of books as a means to knowledge is sanctioned by the university as a part of tradition quite apart from its intrinsic merit.

A professor is caught between defending tradition and embracing innovation. His choices are difficult since neither one nor the other often appears as an unqualified good. The dilemma is described by Donald Morrison in *Memo to a College Trustee:*

> In this conservative atmosphere, the burden of proof is heavily on the proponents of change. In all probability they cannot *demonstrate* that their proposals will have the hoped-for beneficial results. They can gain supporters only by developing an intense commitment and personal dedication to their program. The essential degree of advocacy is difficult for faculty members, who are not zealots by nature or training. Colleagues are likely to respond more positively to un-

derstatement than to exaggeration, and they usually are suspicious of zealots and of utopias. Proponents of change thus face a troublesome dilemma. Unless they have real conviction and enthusiasm for their proposal, they are not able to gain necessary support; but if they are drawn into optimistic claims by the resistance of colleagues, their tactical position is weakened.[6]

An individual may defend the increased emphasis upon foreign languages and yet deplore their being treated as mere instruments of national defense. He may strive for the precision and objectivity of science and still not accord scientific method primacy in all manner of investigations. He may feel sympathetic toward the new grammar, and yet be put off by the new grammarians. At every turn he finds himself required to make discriminations which keep him from allying himself with others for the common but conditional good.[7]

In its daily life as in its formal meetings, the university suffers from the divided attention of its most important group: the faculty. The problems of university government are themselves unsolved because the faculty cannot make university government its principle business. A faculty is ill employed in always looking at itself, but unless it does take a lively interest, the direction of a university passes largely into the hands of administration. Short of individuals suddenly developing virtues which do not come easily to human beings and capacities which are similarly hard to acquire, university government achieves a good deal in being workable if torpid. What should be expected, should be insisted upon, by all within the academic world, is that the attention given to university problems not be annulled by a collective unwillingness to act.

All of these observations point to the difficulty of effecting small changes, the impossibility of effecting consequential changes, in American higher education. At times, American colleges and universities seem determined to learn nothing from the past, apply nothing to the future. It is not that one asks the universities to solve their problems one by one and then use their energies to solve each new problem in its turn. It is, rather, that one expects the universities to use what experience and criticism are intended to teach. Deficient students, teaching, research, and money, the large topics discussed in this section, have provoked much thought, much talk, much writing—and much despair.

What these persisting problems may seem to lead to is *research* in higher education. A national magazine, addressing itself to the deplorable state of writing in American schools, asked a specialist on the teaching of writing (from a College of Education, it should be said) what should be done. "If I had unlimited funds to use in improving the teaching of writing," he replied, "I'd spend money on a massive research program." [8] There's no question that a man to whom "massive" and "research" and "program" come so quickly to mind would spend his money or someone else's on just that. In English, one of the more verbose educational research areas, there is already a ton or more of such research that no one can read, much less make use of. The only thing that the university need do now to make it even more incapable of solving its persistent problems is to embark on a massive research program into its own continued unwillingness to do the things it has long known need to be done.

PART FOUR

Prospects

13. Achievements

WERE it not for the image of generations of commencement speakers presuming to advise millions of college seniors, this book might end here. But since the academic world is fond of talk of any kind and encouraging to all attempts at understanding, the urge to evaluate achievements, to peer into the future, and above all, to present a vision of Utopia, is not only strong but overpowering. What has American higher education achieved? First, a brief look at a number of obvious and impressive achievements.[1]

Most noteworthy, and most verifiable, American colleges and universities have provided higher education for a large portion of society, a larger portion than any other civilization, past or present. In the United States at present, about 1 in 50 of the total population are enrolled in institutions of higher learning. Though an exact comparison is not possible, roughly comparable figures are 1 in 200 in France, 1 in 500 in England, 1 in 90 in Russia.[2]

Second, higher education has enabled an industrial civilization to maintain a high level of existence. It has furnished scientists, technicians, professionals of all kinds in increasing numbers. It has done much to encourage art, music, writing. In short, colleges and universities in America serve a wider range of purposes in our society than in any corresponding technological society. Being able to serve all these ends is a remarkable and too often unacknowledged achievement. America, unlike Europe, had no courtly tradition which passed on to the state the responsibility for maintaining culture. Instead, the universities became centers of culture as well as centers for professional and vocational training.

Third, the university has earned respect as one of the major institutions which not only profess democracy but put it into practice. The colleges and universities have moved steadily toward more democracy in their internal governments rather than less. If the universities, particularly in times of social distress, have advocated measures giving government a larger share of social responsibility, they have also preserved free enterprise as a prevailing academic philosophy. The universities in opening their doors to all have been important forces in enhancing the opportunities of every citizen in a free society. The institutions which have achieved excellence within this democratic framework have shown that *quality* is not inconsistent with *equality*.

Fourth, the universities have been powerful forces for moving America away from provincialism into accepting its position as a dominant country in the world, responsible to all other countries in the world. They have also helped broaden provincial views within the country, helping a rural nation become a cosmopolitan one, helping a nation of disparate individuals become a part not only of American experience, but mankind's.

Fifth, the universities have helped to maintain a persistent and tough American idealism. Secularized as the universities have become, they are no more secular than the society itself. Concerned as they are with the material facts, they expose the students to ideas and ideals with which the society itself is at best only fitfully concerned.

These are considerable achievements. Partly because of them and because of America's dominant position, the American university has become an important place of study for foreign students and a model for higher educational systems in many of the emerging countries of the world.[3] Within a short time the university experience, wasteful, confused, and mindless as it sometimes is, may be the common experience of the majority of American men and women, rather than that of a small minority group as it is elsewhere in the world. If higher learning in America is criticized for falling below expectations, it is partly because it has led critics to expect so much.

If each of the American university's achievements could be regarded as an incontestable good, if each had been achieved to a uniformly high degree throughout American colleges and universities, and if each achievement did not exact its price in weakening the universities in other important ways, the American academic world would surely be the best of all possible worlds. The preceding chapters of this book have looked critically at the particulars of academic existence and practices. The intention of this chapter is to subject the general achievements mentioned above to critical scrutiny.

How incontestable an achievement is the extension of higher learning to a majority of society? The traditions of Western civilization and the steady drift of history would declare that the ideal is central to human aspirations. The only possible objections are those directed toward the ways such an ideal is to be achieved or toward the disregard for limitations implied in the intense belief that the ideal can be realized. American higher education, no more than American society, remembers the essential restrictions that a Puritan theology placed upon man. At every turn, America denies them. Even in the present time of gloomy prospects, our appetite for pie in the sky has been whetted by finding the physical means of getting near it.

Thus considered, the idea of continually expanding higher education may be not precisely wrong, but seductive. The seduction, like the kind most successfully practiced upon women studying for advanced degrees, is one which uses praise of intellect as a means to violation. The attractiveness of increasing the domain of reason is great. The attainment by subjecting the citizenry to an ever-increasing level of formal education is equally attractive. But higher education for all is in a vulnerable position. Either it accommodates itself to lower capacities and loses its character, or it maintains its character and subjects a growing number of students to pointless failure.

For a number of years, the University of Utah has tried to insist upon literacy by requiring that all students pass, in addition to freshman English, an English proficiency test to be taken after their freshman year. The passing mark is the average performance achieved by high school seniors who have taken the same test. If the student fails, he must pass another quarter of English composition before he graduates. A good many students avoid taking the test until senior year, then fail it, take the course, fail that, and begin haunting the halls looking for mercy. The striking fact is not that some of the students fail but that all these seniors, failing or not, have found sufficient courses to make up a major and a minor, have met the other course requirements, and have maintained a "C" average in sufficient number of hours to graduate. Only illiteracy holds them back. As extreme as the example is, it only discloses what everyone suspects: that in every college of an average university, if not in every department, there are those courses which will enable even the dullest to get through.

The University of Utah, according to student opinion, is "easy to get into, but tough to get out of." Like many state universities, it is generous in admitting students and then attempts to maintain standards by failing those who are not up to the pace. But such tactics have an adverse effect upon standards. The more students who fall into this category, the fewer who are likely to be judged strictly. Standards adapt themselves to the clientele; existing courses become easier; easier courses are created; an impossible gap develops between the university's most time-consuming activities and its best work. Students and faculty alike engage in the hypocrisy of feigning higher education while carrying on the work of a secondary school.

Such hypocrisy lends encouragement to the fundamental desires of a majority of citizens to gain a college degree and supports their assumption that it can be achieved through easy and prescribed steps. The consequences might be the development of a model democratic society, somewhat gray perhaps, but satisfied with its grayness. It might also be a society which believed itself to be the highest achievable under a rule of reason only to be constantly betrayed by the unwillingness to stretch its citizens' capabilities, to exercise discipline, and to make distinctions which should characterize any real development of the mind.

The colleges and universities have close at hand the example which might save them the necessity of letting higher education run its course toward becoming universal and universally cheap. The secondary schools have preceded the colleges on the path which higher education is now well along. Between 1870 and the present, the number of students enrolling in the secondary schools and the number graduating have steadily and strikingly increased. The percentage of young people between ages fourteen and seventeen enrolled in secondary schools rose from 7 per cent in 1890 to 84 per cent in 1956.[4] The percentage of youths seventeen years old graduating from high school rose from 1.2 per cent in 1870 to 62 per cent in 1956.

What has been the result? A five-foot shelf of books details the criticisms. The public schools have done too much, taking over chores, responsibilities, and functions which might better have stayed with the family. They have been thoroughly dominated by social usage and life adjustment, concentrating on the students' practical attainments in the world and caring little about an individual's or a society's position in the stream of time. They have diminished the attractiveness of excellence, of working to capacity, of setting up the fullest development of man's intellectual and emotional powers as a foremost aim. They have not developed the conditions, even in a country increasingly able to afford public education and able to profit from it, which make teaching an attractive profession. For students, public school education, whatever its virtues, is too often a tolerably amusing trip through a dreary intellectual landscape. It seems wholly reasonable to confront the colleges and universities with this vista as the territory through which higher learning for all must sooner or later pass. If higher education is to profit from the example of public education it will have to devote at least as much attention to civilizing the land as to populating the territory.

As American higher education has taken in more and more individuals, it has also taken on an increasing number of functions. In this respect, too, the achievement is unmatched elsewhere in the world. The American universities not only provide a liberal education for free men, but are vital centers of culture, research centers, and training institutions for all the professions and most of the skilled technical occupations. The willingness to take on all manner of tasks has kept the universities from becoming exclusively or even primarily intellectual in character. For all that, American society may have gained, since neither tradition nor inclination brought forth other institutions to undertake many of these tasks.

White-collar workers, for whom the practicality and prestige of higher education has a high appeal, became more numerous than blue-collar workers in America for the first time in 1957.[5] The decade 1947–1957 was one of great increase in the number of professional and technical workers, as well as in the number of those in clerical and service occupations. For many of these occupations, college education is not just one way of preparation but the only way, or certainly the preferred way. Throughout the decade, the universities have added new courses of study, new programs, and tailored old programs to meet society's expanding needs. These needs have been artistic and aesthetic—broadly speaking, cultural—as well as technical. Though schools of music, institutes of fine arts, and schools of dramatic arts continue to attract students, the number of individuals being trained in them is much smaller than the number pursuing such studies within the universities. The result is that the universities have become important centers for training artists, actors, writers, and musicians, and for performance of the arts.

Considering the flourishing arts and the high level of technology for national defense as for household conveniences, the American universities have succeeded at both extremes. Being second in space to the Russians, with their obviously greater singleness of purpose, is as much a matter for praise as for criticism. Seeing first-rate theater in a university community may be second to Broadway but that can still be very good indeed. The college graduate has every reason to be satisfied. Having been trained for a professional position, schooled in appreciation of the arts, and being given a steady run of plays, concerts, and athletic events, he might be expected to be more responsive to higher education's continuing cries for support than he is.

From the standpoint of a university's broad aims, the achievement is too impressive to warrant severe criticism. Despite the shortcomings of the curriculum and the course content of that curriculum, the American university at its big best furnishes every occupant with the outlines of a humane culture. Universities are like the great cities of the world: there is far too much going on in them to be experienced by any one student, but every student gains some awareness of the richness of which human society is capable. No undergraduate can quite escape the effects of the expansive life to be found in a modern university, and no one would deny that an engineer given the opportunity to look at paintings, hear classical music, participate in the theater, is the better for it.

If there is any criticism to be offered, it is that the universities often sacrifice their possibilities as educational institutions of one kind in order to be public institutions of another kind. Development of the intellect is the avowed goal of the one; public entertainment is the obvious goal of the other. The announced intention is to balance the two. When such a balance is achieved, the university justifies its dual character by arguing that intellectual development and public entertainment are both needs for which other American institutions do not provide. Athletic divertissements, for example, are defended as responses to public needs which professional sports only partially meet. Team sports, for almost all adults, are vicarious and popular activities. Only within a large, youthful, and unified group can there arise the combination of energies, emotional commitments, and leisure which makes team sports possible. That the public flocks to watch them is not hard to understand; that the university should foster them as public entertainments simply because the culture fails to provide them elsewhere is certainly questionable.

Athletics is, of course, peculiar among university entertainments. Though by now the growth of professional physical education seems to give competitive sports a legitimate place in the university family, they are by-blows of tradition and expediency. Virtually every other university entertainment can be called a contribution to culture, if not precisely a contribution to the development of the mind. The theater lives by performance and relates to history, languages and literature, and philosophy at almost every point. Music and the visual arts are similarly parts of humanistic culture. Each has its justification in the theory of an art, the traditions of its practice, and its close relationship to other academic studies. Such considerations, however, only make them more justifiable university activities than football. The arts as professional entertainments lose their justification when they become substitutes for the disciplined study that is the university's unique responsibility. To put it another way, the university theater may be thanked for keeping the theater alive for a large portion of American people. It may be deplored as it weakens the possibilities for a professional civic theater, and as it diverts the university students from their primary tasks. So may the arts within the university be praised as fostering the arts in the world outside and in providing a place for study and for creation. They may be deplored as they encourage the sole development of a technical, vocational skill as out of place in the university as stenography.

These criticisms gain force when one considers the cost of maintaining the many activities of a modern university. The expenses of providing entertainment—athletic, musical, dramatic, and the like—are considerable. Neither the university nor its public assumes that such activities deserve public support as much as do the central activities of teaching and scholarship. Though the public ultimately pays for both, it tends to forget that the entertainments for which it pays a nominal fee are seldom self-supporting. The citizen sees no inconsistency in complaining about how his taxes are being used to pay for the high life at the university even as he enjoys each of the public gaieties in turn.

There may be no other choice for the universities but to continue serving the public's needs and passions. Perhaps other alternatives would be worse. The wide involvement of the universities in American life has at least been largely independent of direct state control or for that matter of state aims. America has no strong tradition of state support for cultural activities, and private support is aroused by the desire either for participation or for profit. Faced with these conditions, the universities can righteously assume that everything they do is an indispensable service.

The achievement of the universities as institutions fostering democracy has been chiefly in the enlargement of opportunities for an increasing number of citizens, and in the movement toward democratic government and practices within the university. The business oligarchy which Veblen wrote against fifty years ago is not as prominent in universities today. Democracy manifests itself in many ways, from the hopeless equalitarianism of the curriculum to the increased powers of university faculty senates and councils.

The precise effects of the university upon democracy outside the campus are not easily perceived, but its general effects are obvious. Higher education has tended steadily toward widening opportunities for college attendance, and has enabled individuals, through the development of their skills and talents, to make the most of the democratic chance to rise. In both ways, higher education has aided the general movement of this century toward equalitarianism. A higher level of education has meant a more informed citizenry, and more chance of placing educated men in public office. The extension of suffrage, the concern for civil rights, the growth of groups devoted to responsible political action probably owe something to a more educated populace.

At the same time, the universities have not escaped the consequences of emphasizing superiorities of various kinds. The universities are still leading institutions in fostering class distinctions. The attractiveness of the East Coast schools of established reputations will probably always be in part snob appeal, though the demands now being made upon the students at such schools may have the countereffect of forcing graduates to see larger and feel more deeply about the democratic society they enjoy. Intellectual smugness and feelings of superiority are probably more often the outcome of the university experience which offers a demanding intellectual life for the few and a slack-minded high society for the many.

One of the measures of the distance and direction the universities have gone since the thirties is the declining vigor of anti-fraternity voices. Their silence cannot be attributed to any substantial change in the nature of fraternity and sorority life, though increasing enrollments in public, urban, nonresidential universities may have made fraternities and sororities of less national consequence. The fraternity-sorority world is countenanced today because the university has moved in that direction. The university's enhanced physical plant, its preoccupation with money, its teaching of all professional skills and social graces, its attention to the outward signs of culture, its reservations about the value of the intellectual life, its preoccupation with the details of academic and social bookkeeping, are all close to being the values the fraternity system respects.[6] They are not precisely undemocratic values; they are those values widely accepted in the tangible ways they appear in American democratic society: an expensive house, a large income, a professional vocation, a knowledge of the great books, a season ticket to civic music, an orderly schedule of ballet classes, music lessons, and art appreciation for the kiddies, and a clear recognition of how much each costs, how much each is worth.

The social compact by which fraternity membership limits or alters the individual's respect for learning is hostile to the high purposes of a university. Much is lost in submerging individual aspirations in group identity and in defining individual attainments in terms of group ideals and group practices. As a fraternity succeeds in being more than a place of residence (a rationalization for its existence on campus), so does it succeed in being against almost everything the university stands for in the development of a democratic society which prizes the full development of the individual. The identification with fraternity life rather than with university life; the time given over to maintaining a pretentious social life, to accumulating tests, themes, and term papers in fraternity files, to tutoring the stupid and polishing the crude; the excuses that group living gives for human laziness, cheating, and grossness—all these brand the fraternity system as unworthy of its inclusion on the campus.

With university education so widespread, the old distinction between a university man and a nonuniversity man is fading, just as is the distinction between the laborer and the white-collar worker. Where such distinctions are kept alive, it will be in the fraternity system where "college-plus" gets marked off and above "college." Such distinctions do not end with graduation. They continue on in the lives of the growing number of college educated whose tastes are modeled upon those of the fraternity and whose values have the same design. The political lessons learned seem merely to be that power is a prerogative of social position and that democratic responsibility ends with fidelity to one's group.

If these strictures seem intemperate, I quote in full a more restrained conclusion reached by Edward Eddy in his recent book *The College Influence on Student Character:*

> We cannot help but conclude that the fraternity system is a strange anomaly on some college campuses. In many ways it is so close to what the college so often seeks in a dormitory system—relatively small in size, closely knit, and a unit of total education with special responsibility for campus leadership. It offers the opportunity for an unusual maturing process with group idealism balanced by individually held values. . . . Where student needs are met, the student should be expected to devote himself with greater vigor to the intellectual task.
>
> This is what the fraternity could be. It has each of these important potentials—important not just to the membership but to the college of which it should be an integral part. But this is not what was reported to us or what we found, except in several isolated but encouraging cases.[7]

The fraternity system, for all its obvious attractiveness, has repeatedly fallen short of the ideals of academic life. The root cause is surely the sense of special privilege which is hostile both to the democratic sentiments and to that intellectual humility which is the first lesson of higher learning.

The impact of a college student's residential life upon his development as a citizen is probably as important as his classroom participation and his exposure to the wide range of opinions to be found on a college campus. By comparison, the effect of student and faculty governments is small. Enough has been said to indicate my distrust of artificial student democracies whose freedoms end at the administration's decree. The workings of faculty democracy may be downright discouraging, for here, as in other democracies, the constituency is often at the mercy of the uncaring majority and the unyielding minority, and here, too, democracy of great potential excellence often reaches its highest achievement in merely muddling through.

The movement of the universities from provincialism to cosmopolitanism, like the other achievements being discussed here, is not an unquestionable good. Megalopolis may not prove the best habitat for man. Certainly, as one moves from one level of urbanization to the next, there are no clear and unqualified gains which sustain the illusion of progress. Today's dark forebodings are part of the reaction against cosmopolitanism, accompanied, as it of necessity has been, by rising population and the shrinking of space. Less dark and less ultimate are a headful of sentimental beliefs which confront cosmopolitanism with any number of rural golden ages of the past. The most forceful of these beliefs poses the great danger of losing the face-to-face community that was strong in America's rural past.[8] I cannot feel intensely convinced by the argument, nor do I find the university the outstanding force among many other potent forces moving toward urbanism, industrialism, and loss of community. In fact, the university at its best can provide a common culture which serves a portion of the society in somewhat the same fashion as the face-to-face community.

Virtually every college student, in America or out, has experienced the pull away from the home town. And almost as certainly, the colleges have taken youth away and set them down somewhere else, most likely in a suburban development. The worst kind of college experience I can imagine is the halfway one, one which plants the seed of discontent and then never lets it flower. Such, I fear, is too often the experience to be found in halfway universities. Despite the vigorous attempt to retain the student's connection with his native community, enough foreign air gets into his lungs to alter his choice of climate but not enough to let him live in it fully. He becomes a bad journalist, a dilettante politician, a loyal and persistent contributor to the athletic slush fund. Lacking the sense of a large community which a full freedom might have given him, he bewails the loss of the small community or builds an artificial one on the sentimental attachments which university life did provide. He is one of that large group university statesmen worry about—those hardheaded alumni who know that *commencement* is more properly *termination.*

The university is to blame for those it fails to touch, and the number seems to be extremely large. The lesson, to me, is that the universities cannot stop the sophisticating process halfway. The journey of university students from their youthful communities is bound to appear to many as a trip on a straight line away. The university's best hope is to take its students far enough along to show them that the straight line is really an arc that runs through all the communities of man. The further the university can take its students, the more chance they have of realizing they are on an immense circle, not simply on a road away.

If I seem to qualify this achievement of the universities less than the others, it is because the process seems to me inescapable and the universities more successful in answering to it. The growth from rural to urban is not reversible. The universities, even when they are weak in other respects, afford a sense of growth superior to that which arises from the mere multiplication and congregation of numbers. The university experience is the only kind of educational experience other than kindergarten that gives the student a sense of arriving in a new world. Twelve years is too long a time between such experiences; the universities need fear most those advocates of articulation who would make the student's first year of college a mere shift of position at his high school desk.

The American university's achievement in broadening horizons for the individual has been matched by its attention to studying the American experience and America's place in Western civilization. If there is any criticism to offer, it is that the university has come late to realizing the importance of cultures other than European. The recent study, *The University and World Affairs*, asks the universities to "transcend the traditionally domestic and Western orientation of scholarship and training."[9] The study, however, is not suggesting anything of which the universities are not already aware. The commitments of the universities in the last decade to foreign students, to international studies, to research and special projects for foreign countries all over the world, have steadily grown. As yet, enough may not have been done, but the general problem challenges the practical capabilities of the universities and, therefore, is not likely to suffer neglect. Certainly, the university is already a leading force in exposing young Americans to the world outside America and Europe.

The final achievement I have cited is that of fostering idealism in American life. American idealism is a sturdy and oftentimes scrubby growth, chiefly because it draws its sustenance from the barren soil of materialism. Virtually all observers of the American character have noted, in one way or another, the existence of this paradox. Gunnar Myrdal called it "practical idealism." Santayana regarded the symbolic American as "an idealist working on matter."[10] Irwin Edman called attention to the mistake made by those "who are impressed by the American concern with gadgets and practicality and think we are exclusively a literal-minded and practical people." His further remarks are worth quoting:

> But foreigners, on being among us a little while and aware of the half-dreaming aberrations of an allegedly practical people, are quite understandably confused and begin to wonder how practical a people we are. Where else in the world is there such a proliferation of fads and foibles of a naïvely spiritual and idealistic sort? . . . Foreigners weary justifiably at the way in which (an old habit with us) we chant the perfection of our institutions and on the Fourth of July especially make it appear that God's designs have come to full fruition only on this continent.[11]

There is a part of the American character strongly attracted to this shallow but heartfelt idealism. It is that masculine part for whom the schoolteacher is a schoolmarm, for whom college going is effete, for whom the church is for wives and children, for whom business is business. Idealism has rough going, and when it survives in common usage it is in rough-hewn and essentially practical aphorisms like honesty being the best policy or in such vague but powerful ideals as human perfectibility. At its tender worst, it is the spirit of the satin pillowcase with the embroidered "Mother" or the tattooed heart in a trellis of roses.

Idealism that is both more respectable and more hazy is inseparable from education, and the higher the education the higher the ideals. The "happy workmanlike ideals of the American," as Santayana called them, attract because of the possibility that they can be realized. Going to college is one way of realization. The desire for material success is a strong incentive, but students accept materialistic means and materialistic aspirations to satisfy a yearning for some idea of fulfillment beyond satisfaction of their materialistic desires. The university's chief task may be that of keeping alive and vital the ideas and ideals which give strength and substance to such vague aspirations. At no time in its history has the university entirely failed to do so. At certain times it has seemed to succeed more than at others.

As an incitement to battle in World War II, idealism was less a force than in World War I. No former college president defined the purposes of the second conflict as Woodrow Wilson had done for the first: *to make the world safe for democracy*. The slogan the summer before Pearl Harbor was OHIO: *over the hill in October*. College meant a chance for deferment or a way into specialized training or a path to a commission. The war was no adventure; the heroes were not volunteer idealists on a world-saving mission; they were the realist conscripts who did what had to be done out of necessity, fear, and an aching desire to get it over with.

But if idealism was not evident during the war, it became evident in the universities after. There are many explanations for the flood of students into the colleges after the war and for their generally high level of performance. Surely something more was at work than deferred desire, economic opportunism, or drift. One thing was the hardy kind of American idealism which would not embarrass its advocate by bringing him to speak of higher education in idealistic terms, but which would bring him into a university not so much to prepare for a substantial position as to satisfy his unsubstantial yearnings.

There may never be another group as freely motivated and as freely committed to academic life as that postwar group. The G.I. Bill of Rights (its very name borrowed from American political idealism) was one of those remarkable devices in which bureaucratic wisdom approached the divine.[12] Its allotments were shrewdly calculated to relieve gross want without entirely subverting a man's acquisitive instincts. One could live on it, but not well. By working a small number of hours, one could live better and still have free time left for studies. The only academic enterprise that suffered at all was athletics, chiefly because for a half-dozen years, athletes had a chance to be honest men. Given their war experiences, they couldn't easily be seduced, dazzled, or bullied. Given the G.I. Bill allotment, they could play for fun or choose not to play at all.

What the bill inadvertently achieved was the freeing of intellect on a large scale from family pressures, community pressures, even from self-interest. The results were remarkable. Motivation was high, achievement was high, mutual respect between student and faculty was high, and idealism of a hardy, unsentimental kind was high. The commitment to liberal education, for all the wrenching that went on as the crudest war experience was rubbed against academic abstraction, was often intense.

In a central way, these students had undergone the kind of experience most favorable to arousing idealistic feelings. Both bodies and minds had been punished, the one hardened, the other cabined and desensitized, day after day, month after weary month. Sated with brute fact, freed to pursue their desires, the returning veterans had an accumulation of ideals which university experience gave them opportunity to examine. The condition may not soon be repeated, and the present college generation may deserve some sympathy for having had no comparable experience. Today's students have little in their past to bring out any latent idealism. The ever-present fact is a practical, materialistic existence which fills the waking hours. University existence is one of academic routines, now and then relieved by a chance to win artificial distinctions in an academic world. There is fun, and dutiful attendance at lectures by distinguished speakers, and for some, the Peace Corps or freedom-riding in the South. But the absence of a climate favorable to idealism should not blind students to the fact that the colleges and universities still preach idealism of sorts and still have it for any student to draw upon. Nor should the universities fail to be aware that in times like the present they must do a great deal to provide the conditions in which idealism of even a modest kind can flourish.

The achievements of the American university deserve praise and force qualifications in about the same measure and for the same reasons as American society. Nowhere else on earth has man achieved a higher standard of living, a higher level of bodily comfort. And yet, few observers are sure that Americans know what to do with their substance, know how to live. The universities are centrally involved, as unequivocally successful in helping to satisfy man's physical wants as they are dubiously successful in teaching him what to do after his wants are satisfied.

Physically, the academic world is characterized by bigness in as insensible a pattern as in society. On the campus, crowding, bustle, and loss of repose are marked. Within the libraries and the classrooms, more books and more people and less thought. Within the mind, a sense of vastness larger than the teacher's ordinary fear before the vastness of knowledge. Bigness on the campus as in the city has meant a steady loss of the value of the individual as the increased impossibility for any one voice to emerge clearly exacts a willing or grudging submission to the group. Increased size has meant more regulations, more signs to be posted, more overseers to enforce rules, more chance of confusion, and more need for further regulations. Students and faculty conduct their negotiations at long range. In teaching and learning there is often an almost random design. The willingness of men to huddle side by side in row after row of indistinguishable houses is matched by the willingness of students to huddle in undistinguished groups to be filled with negotiable learning. Though the campus still maintains its greenery, the despoiling of the land and the contaminating of the air lurks on the periphery.

Daily life in the academic world is ruled by a materialism not far different from that which turns a profit from all the great mysteries of human life—birth, death, love—the more the mystery, the greater the possibilities of return. Higher education has done well by the central mystery of human learning, and if it does not show a balance sheet as impressive as an insurance corporation's it is only because the educational business was founded on unsound business principles and is still hampered by them today. The goals of students, and the way to them, are close to those of the American world at large. Comfort seems to be the all-embracing aim, of mind as of body. Idealism appears, if it appears at all, as service, particularly that kind which serves both the self and mankind—and in that order.

The values to be found within the university seldom or for long rise higher than those of the community. The eye to the main chance, the scrambling up the ladder, the goal of formally defined, highly paid, and highly publicized success are academically respectable. The shirking of hard obligations like thought and self-discipline and judgment are common. Consistent with its physical expansion, the university now accepts a wider range of timeless truths than ever, not merely the large truths of courage, conviction, beauty, and integrity, but the small ones of withdrawal, compromise, prettiness, and accommodation.

After three centuries of steady growth, the American university does not appear to have lost its essential genius: the ability to adjust to the changing conditions of a dynamic society. Such sensitivity accounts for the variety of institutions within higher education and for the wide variance in their worth. The measure of any one of them differs from any other. All might be measured against that point along the beam of excellence where achievements balance the conditions and practices which qualify them. How many nonstudents and nonstudies can be tolerated by the university before the point of balance shifts too far toward that end? How many public entertainments and campus frivolities dangerously offset the weight of studies? How dense is idealism forced to become to prevail against a corresponding bulk of materialism? In short, how much of all these can the university stand without seriously questioning the worth of intellectual development, weakening the discipline that study demands, and impairing the democracy in which learning flourishes?

14. Drive Versus Drift

THE direction of the American university in the decade ahead will be determined by the drive toward excellence working against the drift toward mediocrity. The words are not mere literary flourishes. At least since Sputnik, there has been a continuing and growing drive toward excellence; no one who has watched the growth of public education in America can be unaware of the drift toward mediocrity. The drive toward excellence is more purposeful and vigorous; the drift toward mediocrity more massive and persistent. The former has the powerful but unsophisticated help of national urgency, the thrust of the physical sciences, and the enthusiasm of college professors. The latter has the steady propulsion of democratic sentiments, the strong desires of large numbers of people, and the aid of all those who fit their course to the path of least resistance.

All American education has been conditioned by the democratic paradox that the society which affords its citizens the greatest possibility of being equal also affords them the greatest encouragement to be unequal. Public education, provided equally for all, has given every man his chance to rise; at the same time, it has tried to check the undemocratic feelings which an intense emphasis upon individual achievements can arouse. The attitude in the public schools toward skipping grades, grouping according to ability, counseling toward intellectual achievement, exempting from routine requirements, even grading by letter or number has varied widely through the years. The dissatisfaction with these practices has behind it not only a criticism of their usefulness, but a suspicion that they are undemocratic. My own public school work, beginning in 1929, was evaluated by letter grades from the first grade on. My children enjoy the benefits of a psychological profile. A number of my older sisters, attending school during the twenties, were permitted to skip grades. By the time I was in the same school, skipping was regarded as bad for everyone. Objections to practices deemed undemocratic in the public schools continue to be made. A high school in a suburban district of Salt Lake City carried on an Advanced Placement Program with difficulty last year because a principal frowned upon the practice of singling out superior students. As a result of such philosophy, the term "exceptional" children no longer means "superior" children, but rather all those who do not fall into the middle range. It is now widely used, a school administrator told me recently, to refer to the subnormal. The "gifted" as a term for those at the other end is causing some distress, and its equivalents—"bright," "upper-level," "talented," "superior"—are no better. Public school administrators will, of course, solve this problem, probably by arriving at some term as vague and as mealy as "enriched."

Right now, the drive for excellence is solidly under way.[1] Books talk about it; conferences discuss it; foundations furnish money to attain it; parents pray for it; students are learning to live with its demands. For the colleges and universities, excellence has primarily meant intellectual excellence. Though intellectual excellence is obviously not the only kind of excellence which human beings should prize, it surely is the highest goal for the specialized efforts of higher education. "The greatest accomplishment in literature, science, statesmanship and a variety of other fields," Dael Wolfle wrote, "is usually associated with very high intelligence." [2] The top range of colleges and universities is confined to those schools which select students for their high measurable intelligence and then make great demands upon them. But these schools are not the ones that are expanding most rapidly. The development of excellence will be of most consequence in the middle range of colleges and universities striving to expand the area of intellectual achievement while still taking care of large numbers of students. An observer watching the development of these schools recognizes their compulsion to emulate those at the top. An ambitious university president knows by now that a thriving graduate program is almost as important as a thriving athletic team. Graduate schools, whatever their defects, place their emphasis almost exclusively upon intellectual excellence. So it is that universities undergoing a gross physical expansion which, on the face of it, seems adverse to excellence of an academic kind, feel compelled to expand the opportunities for the mind as a kind of compensation for not quite being able to slough off their hairy hides.

The state of California affords an interesting example of the movement toward excellence amidst a diversity of educational aims and institutions. The master plan for California schools defines firmly three levels of activity—junior colleges, state colleges, and the University of California—and defines the scope of each as well as the kind of students each may admit.[3] The University of California is declared by statute to be "the primary state-supported academic agency for research." The University has sole authority for awarding doctoral degrees except that it may agree with the state colleges to award joint doctoral degrees in some areas. The primary function of the state colleges, again specified by statute, is "the provision of instruction for undergraduate students and graduate students, through the Master's degree." The junior colleges are open to all students and afford a terminal education as well as the first two years of a degree-program which may be finished elsewhere.

Such a well designed, yet necessarily hierarchical system, is bound to arouse protests. The state colleges, or at least many faculty members in them, are not likely to find full satisfaction in performing the service functions they have been in part assigned. The California system gives only modest encouragement to high intellectual aspirations within the state colleges, and creates a real danger, if the system becomes inflexible, of this middle range of schools becoming intolerably "middle." The highest level of colleges has already achieved in the University of California at Berkeley and at Los Angeles, a very high degree of intellectual excellence. As might be expected, the emphasis in the public institutions of higher learning has had its effect upon private ones. The University of Southern California, for many years long on muscle and short on brains, has set about deliberately to create a new image. Its football rivalry having given it a bogus equality with California and UCLA, it now realizes it must achieve real intellectual distinction if it is to gain real equality.

The development of excellence within those universities which have already assembled the resources and faculties that can sustain the highest kind of endeavor may lead to the rich getting richer, the poor poorer, and the middle more middling. As large universities become larger still, the problems that bigness creates become as pressing for the university as for urban communities. Excellence becomes mixed with many of the more volatile horrors of urban life: the driving of cars; the amassing of bodies; the increasing of noise; the intensifying of competition; the shrinking of judgment; and the waning of space. Considering such probabilities, the quest for excellence seems oddly companioned. Worst of all, time, that most precious of necessities for the work of the mind, gets expended in abusive ways. More and more gets spent on transporting the body from place of residence to place of work or from one place of work to another, on finding a place to eat, a place to relax, a place to live in harmony with one's ideals. The drive toward excellence might be regarded as a less equivocal course if one did not think it involved freeways and interchanges and a resting place in one of those vast parking lots where a mechanical man guards the gate.

The movement toward excellence affects, to some degree, all levels of higher education. Few schools can escape the desire for attaining a degree of intellectual excellence or the signs of it. Programs for the superior student, usually called "honors" or "independent study" programs, exist in several hundred institutions, in small private colleges as well as large state universities.[4] Since 1958, the movement has had its own publication, *The Superior Student*, and reports of various activities comprise a sizable literature. Certainly the movement is praiseworthy, not only in the opportunities it opens up to the superior student but in the reexamination of traditional learning practices which an honors program often requires.

The difficulties of finding a place at the best universities may bring more good students into a wider range of schools, though the number of students at the lower end shows no promise of diminishing. The school in the middle may find much of its energies and its finances going to "exceptional" students at both ends. Further, though bright students and dull students pay the same tuition, bright professors and dull professors don't accept the same salaries. As competition for faculty members increases, the faculty of many institutions will have to be expanded by employing more men of modest abilities and accomplishments. Under such circumstances, honors programs may not receive the wholehearted faculty support they need if they are to serve well.

One hopeful development for all colleges and universities is that the high schools are now seriously engaged in finding and training excellence. Counselors are making students more aware of the need to perform at a high level if they wish to go on to the better colleges. The National Merit Scholarships, too few in number and too competitive in selection, have given stimulation, if not always the right kind of stimulation, to intellectual endeavor in the high school. Many high schools offer special courses for superior students and some are releasing students in their senior year for specific courses at nearby universities. The Advanced Placement Program is a national plan for encouraging excellence in the high schools by giving college level courses in the senior year.[5] Since participating colleges agree to give credit for superior performance in such classes, the program has a direct impact on the colleges. The program, which began in 104 high schools and 130 colleges in 1956, now includes 1200 high schools and 400 colleges.

These activities mean that both the high schools and the colleges are responding to the drive for academic excellence. They also mean that the colleges and universities are going to have to ready themselves for an influx of quality which will tax their resources, challenge the attitudes of their faculties, and raise many questions about university aims and student achievements. At the top range of higher education, the increasingly high level of measurable intelligence in the students and the brilliance of the faculty may create its own difficulties. David Riesman recently observed that "what is happening now in our very top-quality institutions is that many students never attain the very fortunate ability to think that their teachers are stupid, a perception that may be part of their developing competence." He went on to discuss some other adverse consequences: that the gifted students "are pushed and encouraged from a very early age to play from strength rather than weakness"; that they enter college as work-minded and preprofessional as boys whose only goal is vocational training; and that colleges themselves are becoming "preprofessional and protograduate, even if they are liberal arts colleges." [6] In a society which still seems uneasy about intellect, the quest for excellence is not likely to go on without strain. Yet, it seems to be the course the colleges and universities must choose, and even if it is not, it is the course that the conditions in the world today have set them on.

As favorable as the times are to the development of excellence, the drift toward mediocrity will remain powerful. "The numbers game" has become common usage in academic conversation; almost everyone knows something of the population trends which will swell college enrollments in the future. For the faculty, the drive toward excellence is not only animated by their fondness for encouraging high endeavor, but by their contemplating the alternatives—teaching 15 hours of classes to 200 or more students of average competence. Many a scholar is willing to deal with blasé seniors or pedantic graduate students to escape that.

Increasing enrollments favor mediocrity, particularly when the increasing numbers mean more students at a modest level of ability. The colleges are about to find themselves up against the limitations on human development which doom intellectual life in the lower schools to a state somewhat below the high level which critics often assume can be achieved. The presence of incompetent, uninspired, and unintellectual teachers in the public schools is partly the result of having to provide so many teachers for so many students. Nor is educational theory precisely responsible for the domination of American public school philosophy by the idea of equality. In almost all ways, American life in the first half of the twentieth century has become more equalitarian. Incomes, houses, hours and conditions of work, civil rights, occupational opportunities vary less from individual to individual and from group to group with each decade. The Rockefeller report on education foresees in 1975 "a nation both less regionally diverse and more uniform as to living environment." The extension of high school education from a minority of the population to a majority has been a part of this general leveling. College and university training has been similarly extended during a somewhat shorter period of time.

The place of the college of education in a university or of the teachers college in higher education is instructive to those concerned about the drift toward the middle. These colleges are the large islands of mediocrity, not precisely in a lake of purest intellect, but amid islands, large and small, which are more intellectually inviting. The college of education is large because the demand for graduates is large, and because the drift of mediocrity washes up many souls who have given up trying for fairer isles. There are a good many, too, who steer a deliberate course to this destination; others who are aware of no fairer lands, and a few who arrive to regenerate the inhabitants. There are some brilliant students and teachers in the colleges of education, but the nature of intellectual drives and of higher education suggests that a middling competence is the more common characteristic.[7]

The pressure of numbers, the emphasis upon excellence, and the expansion of graduate studies may place the liberal arts college in somewhat the same position as that of the college of education.[8] The liberal arts college may increasingly become the foraging ground for the large numbers of students whose intellectual promise has not drawn them into more specialized areas of study. As the superior student gets excused from the freshman year for work done in high school, as the honors program draws another group away, as the shortage of college teachers makes the faculty not only smaller in size but lower in quality, the liberal arts program becomes like the public high school curriculum. In it are reflected the desires, the previous schooling, and the capacities of the average student. In addition, the attractiveness of the graduate and professional schools and the universities' own tendency to reward specialized excellence, not only draw the best students away from the liberal arts college but also divert the attentions of the best members of the faculty. Excellence becomes that peculiarity of a separate program, or of a specially favored teacher; mediocrity becomes accepted because the pursuit of excellence is going on elsewhere.

At least two other potent forces will further the drift of colleges and universities toward mediocrity: money and the increasing commonness of college education. Education for excellence is expensive. The more talent is identified, the more opportunities are provided for it, and the more colleges and universities prepare themselves to tutor it, the more the total cost of higher education will rise. The ability of superior institutions to attract money is and has always been great. One can find evidence for the attractiveness of excellence in the rapidity with which Harvard achieved its $82,000,000 goal. No school's financial prospects are worsened by a display of excellence, but financial prospects often need to be improved to make excellence possible. With continually increasing enrollments, with competition driving faculty salaries higher, with expansion driving the cost of the physical plant higher, colleges and universities will have trouble meeting the added expenses that accompany improvements in quality. Federal support, when it comes, will come because the colleges have become, in size as well as in importance, vital to the large public interest. The subsurface philosophy which will permit the granting of federal aid is favorable to educational opportunity equally for all. Such financial aid is likely to favor the extending of educational opportunities and the increasing of numbers from among the large middle.

Finally, college education will become even more common in the next decade. The expectation today of a majority of the students in many high schools is that they will go on with some form of advanced education. At a very small and modest high school a few years ago, I listened to the superintendent give out scholarships to over three-fourths of the graduating class. To be sure, not all were for education toward a college degree, and most were for small amounts. Nevertheless, the few students who received no such distinctions will be lonelier still a decade hence. Excellence is not incompatible with universality, but the harmony is strained. A common expectation is likely to be one within the range of common aspirations, zeal, and abilities. Such expectations have had a powerful effect on the public schools; they will continue to have a powerful effect on the colleges. College education will lose some of the useful superiority which goes with being rare.

The conclusions I draw are that excellence in higher education in the years ahead will be no more common than it has been in the past, and the fight to maintain it will be harder. The bodily health of higher education will remain robust, but what goes on in the head will be another matter. In a general way, the enlightenment of mankind seems to have increased progressively century by century. The intense effort toward education for more members of a society and at an increasingly high level may have resulted in a populace which enjoys a higher plane of existence than any previous large civilization. But that is hard to prove. The evidence to be gathered in the way man lives, what he creates, what he destroys, what threats he lives under, what promises he maintains, are not substantial proofs of the victory of educated excellence. One could claim a net gain in the fruits of technology, and in most of the aspects of professional services for which the universities are responsible. As these relate to the core of undergraduate education, the colleges can take credit. More directly, however, credit seems to go to the professional schools and to the exact sciences in the development of their graduate studies, where excellence has always been demanded and the number achieving it comparatively small.

In homely terms, the uneven developments within the academic world mean that reading and writing are going to be badly taught, badly learned, and badly practiced. *Why Joe College Can't Read* may be the popular book of 1971. *Why He Can't Write* could be written today. Why he doesn't know much history, has little philosophy, and reasons chiefly out of comfort and prejudice are questions which will be as pressing then as now. All the same, medical service will be good though costly; rockets increasingly refined but deadly; creature comforts more abundant and gaudy. For it is not likely that events or plans will greatly alter existing patterns of higher education which have emerged from the drift of the past.

Diversity will continue to be the prevailing characteristic. Some institutions will serve the general needs of undergraduate students of average intellectual capabilities. Others will be intended for clearly superior students headed for careers which require advanced study. Others will be graduate schools which maintain, out of tradition or public need, undergraduate colleges. A large portion will be very large universities differing slightly from one another but each embracing a variety of separate schools and performing many functions. The changes that will come about will be small ones. In some ways, separateness of function will be recognized. Graduate schools will probably draw further away from undergraduate colleges. The undergraduate colleges, in turn, may try to draw away from the junior colleges, but more likely, some undergraduate colleges will remain institutions with high standards and the others will be joined by the junior colleges pushing for a higher place. Professional and technical education will remain as it is. It has achieved its necessary excellence; its problem will be that of keeping up with society's needs.

In addition, the colleges and universities will continue to serve a great variety of student and community desires. The attention to student life will not diminish, though it may find itself more at home in the middle range of universities than in those moving to specialized functions. A very great number of vaguely motivated undergraduate students with a dominant concern for social development are necessary to maintain the program of student services characteristic of American universities today. There will be more such institutions, as small institutions grow into large ones and large ones become larger still. As a result, the public may lose most of its self-consciousness, even its suspicions of professors. After all, they will be working out of similar offices, riding the same freeways, consuming the same goods as any other consumer. The family university may come to fill the place left by the disappearance of family devotions and the family doctor.

Whether the public will be better served, whether civilization will profit, is as hard to guess as whether the public, the universities, or the civilization will be around at all. The one guess is not unrelated to the other. Looked at from afar, the drive toward excellence has helped bring man to the edge of peril, and there, even excellence may not save him. Perhaps there is no salvation, just as there is no satisfaction in the undeveloped human condition. The universities justifiably take pride in encouraging man's desire for excellence out of which continually arise the worth and promise of a world less doomed than it presently seems.

15. Hopes and Proposals

LIKE all human institutions dedicated to high purposes, the universities should be more numerous and nearer perfection, and mankind, of course, should respond vibrantly to them. Some of the remarks that follow are exhortations for human beings to be more than human beings commonly are. Some of the remarks, as the tone of this book should have led one to expect, are made with a reckless disregard of probabilities. Some are equally rash about possibilities. Certainly the universities know where they should be going. They have been telling themselves, in articles and books, orations and addresses, for years. Nor have the directions proposed been so varied that the universities have become confused in trying to choose a route. If the universities have gone off in other directions, it may be because of their persistent aversion to taking seriously their own pronouncements about high aims and purposes.

Criticism of American higher education commonly asks that it more adequately meet certain central obligations: to emphasize intellect; to clarify aims; and to lead rather than merely serve.

Debate over these obligations takes the form of specific arguments about strict versus liberal admissions policies, developing the whole man versus developing intellect, vocationalism versus liberal training, community service versus fidelity to truth, science versus humanities, required courses versus electives, general education versus specialization. There is no real hope that American higher education, as a whole, will agree about what obligations are central or about how best to meet them. Any criticism of higher education or a demand for a display of virtue has to be qualified at once by the variety of institutions being addressed. There are institutions now which are as careful in selection of students, as intellectual in character, and as steadfast in aims, as one could desire. They are comparatively few, and almost all are affected by the character of the mass of higher educational institutions. At the same time, they have their effect on the mass of universities which otherwise might have sunk quite beyond the reach of criticism.

These considerations lead me to my first set of hopes: *widening the area of excellence.* I have not discussed in the previous chapter the possibilities of creating new colleges of genuine excellence in order to treat the subject more fully here. The small number of American colleges which uphold the ideal of high intellectual achievement surely can be increased, and the present time provides a favorable climate for the establishing of additional first-rate institutions.

Brandeis University, now just ten years old, furnishes an excellent example.[1] Already, Brandeis has achieved the kind of prestige that enables it to select its student body from eight times as many applicants as can be accommodated. Not coincidentally, the library is the dominant structure on campus. Not surprisingly, the graduate program is being rapidly expanded. Not irrelevantly, there are no scholarships for athletes. One has only to consider the many qualified applicants who could not be accommodated at Brandeis and the large numbers of qualified applicants who are not admitted to other first-rate undergraduate schools to arrive at a sizable number of students ready to enroll in a college which starts with high standards and maintains them.

Nor need a new college fear it could not obtain a first-rate faculty. Brandeis established itself in the very center of academic affluence and by a combination of competitive salaries and wise appeals, secured and has maintained a superior staff. Geography has helped. To the research scholar to whom library resources are a first consideration, the eastern seaboard has a great attraction. The great schools cannot take on the large number of young men who would gladly join their faculties. Thus, a surprising number of nearby colleges are able to achieve, at least for a time, a first-rate faculty. But geography aside, a new college which could offer prospective faculty members good students, high ideals, and an opportunity to put ideals into practice should not have difficulty getting and keeping first-rate teachers and scholars. A new college dedicated to excellence might not have to match the salaries of those many institutions in which quantity constantly threatens quality. It could probably get faculty members for less, and pay them more as the excellence of the college increased its financial prospects. A new college could afford to make bold departures, and its very freedom from tradition should be attractive to young scholars impatient with higher education as it now exists. "I must confess that I have been troubled by what the enthusiastic reception of *The New College Plan* suggests about the state of current thinking about higher education," one of the committee for planning the New College recently wrote.[2] "I am worried about the dearth of new ideas and new plans which this response suggests." [3] The response also suggests that a new college which promised a better brand of higher education should have little difficulty in attracting the men to give that college distinction.

The realities of financing a new college are sufficiently grim to forestall any group of vital young scholars from setting up shop in old army hospitals or abandoned railroad stations. The committee given the responsibility for planning "New College" called it an assignment "to dream big and dream cheap." If the builders could resist the penchant to begin by leveling everything in sight, new institutions might overcome costs by beginning as cooperative ventures of existing colleges, as in the New College plan, or by building on the expiring remains of any of a number of small threadbare institutions. In the resurgence of small colleges, almost a certainty in the face of rising enrollments, excellence should be sought more than mere elevation to a stable mediocrity. Money is certainly the major necessity. Given purpose and money a good many small colleges could emerge as larger institutions of genuine excellence. Here is an opportunity for the foundations; their special contribution, supposing money was forthcoming, would be to ascertain the wisest place to establish a college and what kind it should be in relation to its surrounding institutions. The zeal which caused so many colleges to spring up in the past century should be replaced by wisdom in establishing new colleges today. The establishment of even one first-rate college could have an effect as beneficial to higher education as that of improving quality slightly in a large number of existing institutions. A college's deficiencies drive their own spur, and higher education as a whole might be better served by getting the horse into a new stable than by merely padding the stall.

The New College plan just mentioned, Michigan State's experimental college at Oakland, Wayne State's Monteith College, and experimental programs at Hofstra, Antioch, Oberlin, Wesleyan, Goddard, Bard, and elsewhere, indicate a strong interest in finding new ways to widen the area of excellence. A part of such interest could well be directed toward reviving the idea of a national university.[4] From 1776 to the present, a federal university has had many strong advocates, including Washington,

Jefferson, Madison, and John Quincy Adams. Higher education is a national interest. The state universities and their near-relatives, the land-grant schools, have become national universities fully as much as state ones.

The establishment of a first-rate federal university could be of great value in furthering the high aspirations of higher learning. It could demonstrate that the national government has a stake in higher education and an ability to support it without control, and in so doing, obligate congressmen to exercise much restraint and demonstrate a good deal of wisdom. Though such a university could become a blunt instrument for state power, there is little reason, arguing from the present character of American governmental and academic institutions, to think it would. If it chose to follow the pattern of state universities, its board of trustees could be chosen from men of such high intelligence and achievement as virtually to assure wisdom in its policies. If it modeled its internal structure upon the democratic principles already outlined and in existence in the great private universities, it would be a model of free inquiry not to be excelled by any democratic institution. If it remained, as the Supreme Court remains, above sectional interest and rivalries, political bargaining and state policy, it could become an institution magnificently declaring itself for the life of reason as the Supreme Court declares for the rule of law. Even now, the United States has three large academies and a number of smaller ones for training the military. Is training for peace any less urgent, and is the national interest any less to be served by an institution whose ultimate purpose is peace, and whose rule of discipline is freedom of inquiry? The Free University of the United States of America, as it might be called, could exert great power, not only in exemplifying principles but in operating as a university in the interests of free men, which, in a democratic country, are the highest interests of the state.

My second set of hopes is for *decreasing the distance that separates the best institutions from the worst.* Suggestions about decreasing this distance are implicit in the previous chapters, and what is said here about consolidation and cooperation proceeds from those implications. The importance of pulling up the bottom has been recently discussed by Everett C. Hughes as a matter of increasing morale to enable the faculty "to keep up a good pace of work themselves and to set up a good pace and standard of work among their students." "There are hundreds of institutions in this country," he went on, "where no education on a high level is going on and where the teachers hardly touch at all the orbits where such work is done." [5]

There is a real danger, now that expanding enrollments are pushing out into even the weakest colleges, that such colleges will feel their existence more justified by the growing number of students they serve. Thus, with no change in quality, they become larger, more stable, and more consequential a part of higher education. There is, as I have said, a relationship between size and quality. Without a very large endowment, a small school cannot operate at a level of efficiency which can maintain a good faculty, adequate libraries and laboratories, and the conditions favorable to excellence. Such a college, growing larger, experiences some immediate affluence from the effects of more tuition income and relatively little more expense for faculty and buildings. Once, however, the balance between faculty and physical equipment, on the one hand, and students, on the other, reaches a point of operating efficiency, growing large does not mean getting richer, nor does it mean getting better. That rests with the aspirations of the college and the ability to fulfill those aspirations. Small colleges grown large are not doomed to mediocrity. But considering the number of them, the increasing difficulties they face in finding adequate support, and the increasing competition for faculties and students, even a defender of the old school might admit they need help to escape that fate.

The need for consolidation is obvious. The way to it is difficult. Indeed, the difficulty increases as larger enrollments give the small colleges a show of life. The combined efforts of boards of trustees, administrations, and faculty are often not able to move a college from its place of birth or to merge one college's sacred identity with another's. The past gives no precedents to speak of, although consolidation of public schools has been going on, even against protest, for at least half a century. In state-supported systems of higher education, coordinating councils to examine and pass judgment on over-all educational needs have been a conspicuous development of the past decade. Suggesting a master plan for consolidation of private institutions or even suggesting standards by which the need could be measured would serve only to arouse antagonisms. I leave the idea, therefore, as it is, a pious hope sneakily dropped into the conversation.

A tangential approach is open, and is becoming reasonably common. This is the approach of cooperation. "It could easily be shown," Lotus Coffman, president of the University of Minnesota, wrote in 1931, "that the refusal on the part of higher institutions of learning to consider the allocation of function results in inefficiencies and mediocrity." [6] Since that time, sharing of resources, defining of functions, and allocating of responsibilities have increased. The Claremont colleges of California are a consequential example.[7] The lot of many small colleges could be improved by similar affiliation, and such affiliation could be the first step toward relinquishing institutional self-interest which, in turn, might lead to consolidated colleges. President Coffman has put the matter forcefully, succinctly, and with the necessary qualifications:

> When the colleges and universities of America free themselves from that fetish of respectability which requires them to offer instruction that their neighbors are offering; when they cease to compete for the purpose of salving their consciences; when they decline to appeal for money because someone else has something; when they

discard that selfish tradition to which they cling and before which they worship—the tradition that those colleges are best which present the greatest variety of offerings—then college and university instruction in America will be conducted on a higher plane than ever before.

One last idea emerges from this consideration of improving the lower level of American higher education. Raising that level somewhat might bring such schools close enough to the respectable universities that an exchange program among American institutions could become possible. Even now, there is some exchange of faculty members between institutions of comparable salaries and standards. A university professor from Stanford is not unwilling to spend a summer at the University of Colorado. Even Harvard professors, at least retired ones, have been found as far south and west as Texas. But distinguished professors, active or retired, cannot be easily persuaded to trade a year at a major university for a year at Washoe College.

A domestic Fulbright program may be out of the question during a time when the professors have more attractive destinations, but the idea is worth implanting now. The distance between the worst and the best needs diminishing. If the bottom were to rise somewhat, at least in hummocks and hills, those on top might more willingly journey down. The presence of a first-rate scholar-teacher at a mediocre small college is an immediate and consequential way of enlarging that college's vision. If the man he replaces spends his year on the heights, he may return a new man a year hence. A continuing passage between the levels of academia could not help but improve the prospects at the lower level and should not work great harm at the upper.

Such a program, like consolidation, involves some sacrifice of individual desires, some breach perhaps in institutional solidarity, some danger of alien ideas arising in one place as another. But it seems an easy and effective way of working toward higher education of a more uniform excellence. If this kind of cooperation and transfer were to help unseat prejudice and sentiment, that would be an additional gain.

My third set of hopes concerns *professors and administrators.* The time has long passed when their mutual dependence and the university's needs should have made them wise collaborators in the university's destiny. The time is at hand when, the fiercer conflicts having abated, the two could make common assault on the university's ills. Chiefly, this involves a closer look at the structure of university government, some relinquishing of rights and prerogatives by both parties, and a willingness of the faculty to accept and the administration to permit larger faculty participation in university government.

University government as it affects policy of the university depends heavily upon the faculty. Though the faculty has been drawn into policy-making more and more in the past fifty years, it still finds its own habits and the resistance of administrators an excuse for inaction. The temper of the "new professors," as Robert O. Bowen's recent book calls them, may be more aggressive than that of professors in the past. Even so, revisions in university government will have to be made if the universities are to profit from new ideas and new attitudes.

Faculty councils or senates are now widely accepted as necessary to any university government. They are usually elected bodies which meet at regular intervals and with members of the administration as ex officio members. They have some degree of authority over almost all matters affecting the curriculum, can study or debate almost any question involving the life of the university as a whole, and are sometimes able to translate the faculty will into university policies and practices. The presence of a faculty senate, its strength and effectiveness, is not only a measure of the degree of faculty participation in university government but a rough measure of the general excellence of the university. Institutions that do not have them need to seek them; institutions that have them, need to make them better.

The method of selecting members of a faculty council is a place to begin. Following established procedures in civil government, the universities usually select council members according to colleges, areas, and departments. The size of the constituency determines the number of representatives. Nominations are made, names placed before the faculty, and elections achieved by secret ballot. Insofar as these general practices are followed in a democratic fashion, they seem to be model practices. There is, however, one serious objection. University democracy is not so precisely similar to a political democracy that vital practices can be taken over without change. The university has no party system; elections arouse no campaigns, no oratory, no publicity but word of mouth. The consequence is that places on a faculty council tend to go to the men who have served longest and are, therefore, well known. A council composed of such men is likely to be both conservative and provincial, and the fundamental need to see a university in a context larger than its own peculiarities escapes the attention of the representative body whose vision should be most broad.

Thus, there is a real need for a faculty senate to look to its method of selecting members if it wishes to be a vital force in a university's continuing policies. Instead of accepting natural selection, it should go out of its way to provide for unnatural selection. By careful attention to apportionment, the faculty could ensure the play of youth against age, of outsiders against locals, of the lower academic ranks against the upper, of one kind of academic background against another. It cannot bring into its senate the broad range of vital opinion existent in a faculty by selection according to mere number and familiarity.

A related matter and one of equal importance is the presence of ex officio members in the faculty senates. The practice is a bad carryover from university oligarchy. Democracy affords little warrant for this widely accepted practice. Free discussion is free only among equals. There are too many matters which a faculty member cannot or will not discuss freely before his dean or his department head or before anyone who has authority over him. The notion that the ideally administered university is one in which a faculty member can speak his mind freely before any member of the administration is humbug. Such a claim falsifies human nature even as it seeks to praise the exceptional qualities of men in power. The deans, the alumni representatives, the president, the vice presidents must go; a faculty senate which has not won the right to deliberate alone is operating well below its potentialities.

I have chosen to pick out specific weaknesses in the makeup of faculty senates because I feel strongly that the hope for university statesmanship rests with such bodies, and such bodies in turn have the possibilities of making their actions more statesmanlike. All other hopes for better university governments address themselves to improving the nature of human beings and institutions. They involve exhorting faculty members to stop acting like pork-barrel politicians, to face their own weaknesses and relinquish their total right to protect them, to examine their own disciplines as critically as they examine those disciplines they dislike, and to insist upon being given responsibilities in directing the course of the university. Similarly, one must exhort administrators to aim higher than expediency and to resist the temptation to consolidate and wield all power. Administrations must be urged to lift some of the secrecy which protects the details of the business operation, including budgets, athletic expenses, and salary scales. They should be encouraged to make their dealings with the trustees much less private business and much more public business of concern to trustees, administrators, and faculty alike. Until these hopes are somewhat realized, the highest form of university government may be that in which the president of necessity runs the show but lets the faculty members think they are running it themselves.

My last set of hopes is a set of bold proposals addressed to academic life as it goes on day after day. There is nothing wrong with the principles of the universities that putting them into practice would not improve. The following is addressed to practices. The author acknowledges that few academic men would subscribe to the principles which apparently underlie the practices being attacked. Few academic men would admit responsibility for the practices. Since no one is to blame, no one can be addressed, and these proposals are the mere burst of oratorical fervor left over from my labors. Like the round of congratulations for the hard work of the committee, they are not meant to be taken seriously.

First, the end of athletics. I do not mean here, the end of recruiting, or point-shaving, or archery. I mean the end of physical education within the college, the end of B.A.'s, M.A.'s, Ph.D.'s in the subject, the end of coaches and trainers and rubbers and experts on the metatarsal, the end of stadiums and fieldhouses, and the beating of baseball bats into pencils. Short of this, I see no hope whatsoever that a rule of reason can prevail in the conduct of intercollegiate sports.

What would take its place? With the size of the American campus, with the deadliness and clutter of automobiles, putting autos on the outside and the student on his feet from the parking lot to the classroom would keep his mind free and his body trim. If the universities are willing to do that, a slight concession can be offered. Physical education is allowed on the fringes of the campus, and on the way to more serious business, the student stops to learn tennis, basketball, and the lifting of weights. The exponents of such skills set up their stalls, bark their wares, and charge by the hour. The university, having learned how easily faint inclinations become obsessive desires, erects a wall or a moat or a tangle of barbed wire to separate the lower sphere of activity from the higher.

Second, the end of fun. I am no more opposed to fun than to physical exercise. It is to be prized, and every passing year which subtracts from the pleasures of either is among life's solemn losses. But since such pleasures are prized, youth will seek both out. If fun has to be taught, has to be administered, has to be assigned rooms and credit hours, it has lost its essential character long before it is put in the catalogue. So, out with the ministry of fun. If it wishes to set up its consultation booths, its boxes of bunting, its competitive enterprises out on the edge with the athletes, let the civic authorities regulate its traffic. But should it try to sneak inside, then the university must enact and enforce the necessary zoning laws.

If a university could get rid of the professional gamesters and the promoters of fun, it might even set up recreations of a sort on the campus proper. Large patches of greensward with boxes of bats, balls, gloves, rackets, put in small sheds out of the weather would suffice for physical education and double for fun. Shrubs, trees, brooks, should be there for other kinds of relaxation. And if immorality increaseth as does the clock's hours, then spotlights do as much as housemothers. But with the end of the ministry of fun, who is to worry whether the lights are on or not?

Third, the end of nurtured mediocrity. A fundamental rule should be adopted throughout the land. *No higher educational institution should exist without some standard of admission.* This does not mean the standard should be the same for all, or even that it should be very high for some, but it means that it should, without exception, exist. I have never heard more than two defenses for a lack of standards. The first is that in the state-supported schools, state constitutions require admission of all students of whatever description. Few state constitutions do not qualify that statement by adding such phrases as "properly qualified students," or "to the degree that the student can profit." No state constitution requires that all students in state-supported schools must pass. The second defense is no defense, but a plea of need: that one student's money is as good as another's, whatever his academic abilities. Certain wellings of sentiment give support to these arguments, but these sentiments are more characteristic of lower school educational philosophy than of higher.

When I was a high school boy thinking about attending a state university (which I found out twenty years later admitted everyone), it was common, if inaccurate, knowledge among my peers that the university was tough to get into. We suffered little from it; we respected it more; we worked so that we might get in; and we often went on to the state university because being accepted there was an achievement almost as satisfying as acceptance by an important school in the East. In the minds of the students I now encounter, the psychology has changed. No one fears he won't get into a college or university. Some fear they may end up taking three bonehead courses in summer, but bonehead arouses neither fear nor awe. In some schools, it can become a sizable college career in itself. The change, it seems to me, is the pernicious consequence of an educational philosophy in which standards and democracy have become hopelessly confused and have not yet become untangled. The lesson must not be lost on the college. That which we gain cheaply, we value lightly. The argument for standards rests firmly on that.

Fourth, the end of grading and with it the scrapping of most of the machinery of academic bookkeeping. No one can say the times are particularly favorable to this move. Increasing enrollment is a challenge to which the university's genius for management responds. Nevertheless, grading might as well go one time as another. Grades are chiefly useful in providing an incentive, but if the universities cannot find better incentives than this, they deserve the students' indifference. Aside from that, grades merely facilitate the movement of a student unable to make it at one place to a place where he can.

How to get rid of grades and credit? Simply start an academic year without them. Every university is engaged in an extensive initial testing program, in which the Predicted Grade Point Average approaches the omniscience of Divine Wisdom. Since it is based upon the achievements of twelve years of previous education and upon a battery of tests which reflect the effects of living seventeen or eighteen years, as well as the accumulations of formal schooling, the omniscience is not mere illusion. It is an accurate enough measure to be entered in the registrar's books opposite each student's name. If it is high enough to get him admitted at all, it is high enough to become the university's bond which can be cashed in for a B.A. or B.S. degree if the student puts up with what the university will require of him over a four-year span. In one gesture, the grading and credit system is swept away, and it is hard to see that the ends of American university education have been adversely affected.

Once having made the central admission that the university awards its degrees chiefly for sticking it out, the university could make other changes intelligently. Genuine incentives could then appear. A student wouldn't be writing five vapid term papers in five unrelated subjects for either the gentleman's C or the grind's A. The student worthy of being called that might be writing one paper in two years which demonstrated not merely his rates of absorption and retention and regurgitation but his power of mind. The rewards should be substantial, as heart-warming as cold cash, for example, and the opportunities for them plentiful. There might even be examinations, not the kind that have to be taken at the eleventh hour and passed with a C— for graduation, but real examinations. If the man gets to the eleventh hour, he's still holding the university's signed bond, and there need be no monkey business, as there is now, about how to award him a degree even though he's still inadequate. He'll be so whether he gets the degree or not, and the university need not be so hypocritically high-minded about it. It's not the mere bond-cashers that deserve examination anyway. It's those who want an examination, and who have earned it by performance all the way along. For them, the examination is not scanned by a machine but judged by a human mind. It becomes a measure for the individual of his powers and for the society, too, if a record of performance seems necessary.

The result is that just as many mediocre students get B.A. and B.S. degrees as before, but a vast amount of faculty time and additional expense is saved in the process. That time and money go into improving the education of those who have not been counting up credits but who have been trying to acquire wisdom.

Finally, what might be a natural consequence of all the rest, the end of hypocrisy. The disparity between what the American universities profess and what they practice grows with the growth of the universities. The style of utterance is not as orotund as it once was, but the substance is still the conventional piety which arose at the laying of the first cornerstone and which will last until the awarding of the last diploma. The practices have been the subject of this book. Only an institution with a head full of noble sentiments could talk so grandly of higher learning and be so tolerant of low performance, be so concerned with discipline and provide so many ways to avoid it, be so enamored of research and so unmindful of pedantry. Despairing of changing practices, the universities might try chastening their rhetoric. They might talk less about their high morality and more about the corruption that feeds on sportsmanship; less about their nurturing the mind and more about their bland exploitation of the body; less about their defense of the liberal studies and more about the ways the universities merely confirm prejudice and certify respectability.

American society has given the university large responsibilities. It has asked them to continue with the civilizing task which falls to all education, the making of "children and youngsters, half-animal and half-savage, into human beings." [8] It has also desired what the universities' traditions insist upon, the disciplined development of the mind beyond the reach of the mass of men. The universities have tried to do both: civilize without cheapening the value of thought, and educate at a high level of aspirations without demeaning the intrinsic worth of every human being.

The social character of an American campus, for all its show and for all its triviality, is not without its real splendor. The poorly endowed and poorly prepared are drawn to the colleges because they recognize the attractiveness of the life that goes on there and have some glimmer of the larger life to which university education may lead. Few who enter the university fail to feel the sense of man's high purpose, fail to perceive a pattern of life in which richness and grace exist in harmony with discipline and dedication. Few fail to profit from the exposure.

For all that, the universities jeopardize their very power to attract and excite if they do not remain true to their main task of freeing and disciplining the mind toward the acquiring of knowledge and the growth of wisdom. The differences in men and women on the brink of maturity must be recognized wisely—not sentimentally, harshly, or idly—but they must be recognized. There is no easy way for a man to reconcile his capacities with his desires; that fact cannot be blinked nor the university's character compromised in refusing to accept it. Civilization moves from lower to higher degrees, and its path follows the disciplined development of the mind which has always been the university's main concern.

NOTES

INTRODUCTION

1. Dael Wolfle, *America's Resources of Specialized Talent* (New York: Harper, 1954), pp. 1–9, gives an idea of the importance of educated manpower.
2. The Educational Policies Commission, *Higher Education in a Decade of Decision* (Washington: National Education Association, 1957), pp. 70–72.
3. The estimate of one-fourth (the exact figure is probably nearer 23 per cent) was arrived at by using the fall enrollment for 1961 of degree-credit students in higher education against an estimate of the population ages 18–24 based on census figures. See Office of Education, Department of Health, Education and Welfare, *Opening (Fall) Enrollment in Higher Education, 1961: Institutional Data,* Circular No. 637 (Washington, 1961). The 18–24 age group is a more realistic age group for college students now, though it probably was not when the Office of Education first started compiling these figures in 1870. See *Statistics of Higher Education, 1955–1956: Biennial Survey of Education in the United States, 1954–1956,* Chapter 4, Section 1, Table III, p. 8, for complete table of growth. The statistics on percentage of college-age population are tricky ones; some of the problems are suggested in the next note.
4. The percentage of the college-age population going to college is variously estimated for the period after World War II. One set of figures for 1950 hovers around 30 per cent. Another set, which omits the veterans as an unwarranted addition to enrollments, gives around 20 per cent. Projecting forward from such a shaky basis makes percentage figures for the future something of a guess. However, both statistics and informed opinion support the belief that the percentage of college-age youth who go on to college will continue to rise. See Bernard Berelson, *Graduate Education in the United States* (New York: McGraw-Hill, 1960), pp. 71–73, for a discussion of the difficulties of arriving at an accurate figure.
5. Office of Education, Department of Health, Education and Welfare, *Residence and Migration of College Students, 1949–50,* Misc. No. 14 (Washington, 1951), p. 3.
6. Coordinating Board of Higher Education, *A Proposed Coordinating Council of Higher Education for Utah* (Salt Lake City, 1958), p. 37.
7. Statistics about numbers and kinds of institutions are from Office of

Education, Department of Health, Education and Welfare, *Education Directory 1960–1961, Part 3: Higher Education* (Washington, 1960), and *Biennial Survey, op. cit.* The information in the following paragraph refers to degree-granting colleges and universities.

8. If the junior colleges are included, about 56 per cent of the students enrolled in higher education were in public institutions in 1957–1958. If they are excluded, the figure is about 54 per cent.
9. See "The Diversity of the System," in John W. Gardner, "How to Think About College," Annual Report of the Carnegie Corporation of New York, 1957, p. 6.
10. Robin Williams, Jr., *American Society* (New York: Knopf, 1951), p. 282.
11. John Henry Newman, *The Idea of a University* (Rinehart Editions 102, 1960), p. 76.
12. *Ibid.*, p. 92.
13. David Riesman, *Constraint and Variety in American Education* (Garden City: Doubleday Anchor Books, 1958), p. 33.
14. Alfred North Whitehead, *The Aims of Education and Other Essays* (New York: Mentor Books, 1949), p. 26.

Chapter 1: LIMBO

1. Lloyd P. Williams, "Quiescence, Tradition, and Disorder—Cross-Section of a Small College," *AAUP Bulletin*, XLIII (December, 1957), 624–625.
2. The wording of the Northwest Ordinance of 1787 is "Religion, morality, and knowledge, being necessary to good government and the happiness of mankind, schools and the means of education shall forever be encouraged."
3. An extreme example of a low level of ability in the freshman class of an accredited American college is given in W. Max Wise, *They Come for the Best of Reasons—College Students Today* (Washington: American Council on Education, 1958), p. 18. College A used the American Council on Education Psychological Examination as part of its freshman testing program. Scores were so low, however, that tests of reading ability and mathematics commonly used in the public schools were substituted. The mean level of scores made by two entering classes in reading was at the fifth grade, sixth month; in arithmetic at the fifth grade, eighth month.
4. Letter from David Bourns to Editor, *Presbyterian Life*, July 15, 1961, pp. 4 and 36.
5. "Faculty-Administration Relationships: Monmouth College (New Jersey)," *AAUP Bulletin*, XLVII (March, 1961), 5–23.
6. See Lloyd E. Blauch, *Accreditation in Higher Education* (Washington: U.S. Government Printing Office, 1959); "The Professor and Accreditation: A Panel Discussion," *AAUP Bulletin*, XLVII (June, 1961), 146–150.
7. William Rainey Harper, *The Trend in Higher Education* (Chicago: University of Chicago, 1905), p. 377.

8. James Bryant Conant, *The American High School Today* (New York: McGraw-Hill, 1959), pp. 37–38, 76–85. Dexter Keezer, ed., *Financing Higher Education: 1960–70* (New York: McGraw-Hill, 1959), p. 44: "There is not much excuse on economic grounds for colleges of less than 1,000." See also William W. Hall, Jr., *The Small College Answers Back* (New York: Richard R. Smith, 1951). The College of Idaho in 1940 set 500 as the ideal enrollment. See discussion of some of the problems of size, pp. 95–97.
9. John D. Millett, *Financing Higher Education in the United States* (New York: Columbia University Press, 1952), pp. 91–92.
10. *Biennial Survey of Higher Education in the United States, 1954–1956.*
11. Burges Johnson, *Campus versus Classroom* (New York: Ives Washburn, 1946), p. 33.
12. Department of Health, Education and Welfare, *Residence and Migration of College Students, 1949–50,* Misc. No. 14 (Washington, 1951), p. 3. Iowa was 26th among the states in 1949–1950, 158 college students per 10,000 population.
13. See Hall, *The Small College Answers Back.*
14. Office of Education, Department of Health, Education and Welfare, *Library Statistics of Colleges and Universities, 1959–60, Part I: Institutional Data* (Washington: U.S. Government Printing Office, 1961).
15. "The Economic Status of the Profession, 1960–61," *AAUP Bulletin,* XLVII (June, 1961), 101–134.

Chapter 2: Purgatory

1. It probably does not need to be pointed out that the state universities, as a group, fit into this category. The books about them are many. Some authors might put them near the top of Purgatory; others near the bottom. See Lotus D. Coffman, *The State University: Its Work and Problems* (Minneapolis, University of Minnesota Press, 1934); Norman Foerster, *The American State University* (Chapel Hill: University of North Carolina Press, 1937); and James L. Morrill, *The Ongoing State University* (Minneapolis: University of Minnesota Press, 1960).
2. W. Max Wise, *They Come for the Best of Reasons* (Washington: American Council on Education, 1958), p. 25: "Their life plans include an early marriage, three or four children, a happy home, leisure for social activities, sports and the development of a hobby or two, a modest amount of activity in the public affairs of the community—and a job that is secure, fits their capabilities, is enjoyable and satisfying, and provides sufficient means for them to carry out the rest of their plans. Beyond this they generally do not aim."
3. Coffman, *op. cit.*, p. 205. He intended the remark to be complimentary.
4. Abraham Flexner, *Universities: American, English, German* (New York: Oxford, 1930). Dr. Flexner's observations about social service, correspondence courses, and curriculum drew heavily upon practices at the University of Chicago and Columbia University. As David Riesman has pointed out, these institutions and others like them have by now moved

to a high plane, and the abuses to be found there thirty years ago are now commonly found in the state universities aspiring to a high level.

5. Office of Education, Department of Health, Education and Welfare, *Academic Degrees,* Bulletin 1960, No. 28 (Washington: U.S. Government Printing Office, 1960). This bulletin lists more than 1600 different degrees currently being conferred by American institutions of higher education. Engineering has 350; education, 250; business, 175. Spurious and junior college associate degrees aside, the degrees given show a wide range of possible occupations. Legitimate B.A. or B.S. degrees are to be had in Real Estate, Recreation, Sanitary Science, Police Science and Administration, Landscape Operation, Restaurant Management, Group Work Education, Family and Community Living, Agricultural Journalism, Engraving, Fabric Design, and Human Relations. Spurious degrees extend the range by preparing graduates to become Practitioners of Truth, Philosophers of Truth, and Doctors of Divinity in Bio-Psycho-Dynamic Religions.

Chapter 3: PARADISE

1. Bernard Berelson, *Graduate Education in the United States* (New York: McGraw-Hill, 1960), makes the most recent and most thorough examination of the graduate schools which are the leading institutions and the leading force at the top level of higher education.
2. See recent series in *Harper's* by David Boroff. The series includes schools other than those at the top level, but the first article was, as one might expect, "Imperial Harvard," October, 1958, pp. 27–34.
3. Berelson, *op. cit.,* pp. 124–128, contains a brief, informative discussion of rating institutions according to quality. He classifies universities into the top 12, the next 10, and a third group of 27, and liberal arts colleges into a "best" group of 48, a "better" group of 70, and a third group of the rest.
4. Robert O. Bowen, ed., *The New Professors* (New York: Holt, Rinehart and Winston, 1960), pp. 61–62.
5. Spencer Klaw, "The Affluent Professors," *The Reporter,* XXII (June 23, 1960), 16–25.
6. Margaret Mead, "Marrying in Haste in College," *Columbia University Forum,* III (Spring, 1960), 32.
7. Philip Jacob, *Changing Values in College* (New York: Harper, 1957), pp. 99–116. "Potency to affect student values is found in the distinctive climate of a few institutions, the individual and personal magnetism of a sensitive teacher with strong value-commitments of his own, or value-laden personal experiences of students imaginatively integrated with their intellectual development." P. 11.
8. Berelson, *op. cit.,* pp. 93–101.
9. Seymour Harris, "Who Gets Paid What," *The Atlantic,* May, 1958, pp. 35–38.
10. See David Riesman, *Constraint and Variety in American Education* (Garden City: Doubleday Anchor Books, 1958), pp. 25–65.
11. *AAUP Bulletin,* XLVII (June, 1961), p. 150.

12. In meetings held during the past five years, the TEPS group has invited representatives from subject-matter fields in the liberal arts colleges and universities to discuss matters of importance to higher education. Nevertheless, the organization is still primarily associated with and led by faculty members from teachers colleges or colleges of education. The journal of the Commission for Teacher Education and Professional Standards, *The Journal of Teacher Education,* is written largely by teachers of education and reflects the aims and tones of the organization.

Chapter 4: THE PECULIAR PROFESSION

1. A number of books which give insight into the life of the professor are: Logan Wilson, *The Academic Man* (New York: Oxford, 1942); Claude C. Bowman, *The College Professor in America* (Philadelphia: University of Pennsylvania, 1938); Jacques Barzun, *The Teacher in America* (Boston: Little, Brown, 1945); Theodore Caplow and Reece J. McGee, *The Academic Marketplace* (New York: Basic Books, 1958); Robert O. Bowen, ed., *The New Professors* (New York: Holt, Rinehart and Winston, 1960); Paul F. Lazarsfeld and Wagner Thielens, Jr., *The Academic Mind* (Glencoe, Ill.: The Free Press, 1958).
2. U.S. President's Commission on Higher Education, chairman George Zook, *Higher Education for American Democracy* (Washington: U.S. Government Printing Office, 1947), Vol. IV, p. 16.
3. Herbert E. Longenecker, "University Faculty Compensation Policies and Practices in the United States: a Study of the Policies, Practices, and Problems Related to Supplemental Compensation of University Faculty Members" (Urbana, Ill.: University of Illinois Press, 1956), has a discussion of such part-time occupations and their effect upon the profession.
4. Troy L. Middleton, President of Louisiana State University, in Longenecker, *ibid.,* pp. 22–23.
5. Joseph S. Roucek, "The Status and Role of American and Continental Professors," *The Journal of Higher Education,* XXX (May, 1959), 260–265.
6. Bernard Berelson, *Graduate Education in the United States* (New York: McGraw-Hill, 1960), pp. 69 ff., discusses the numbers of college teachers needed and the prospects for finding them.

Chapter 5: "STUDENT LIFE"

1. Characterizing college students is one of the standard exercises for national magazines as well as for professional journals. A year does not go by that one magazine or another does not decide that this year's students are more supine or more active, more verbal or more silent, more moral or more wicked, than last year's. The professional journals of those engaged in mothering and fathering the students are as rich in content if not too readable. The booklet cited previously, W. Max

Wise, *They Come for the Best of Reasons* (Washington: American Council on Education, 1958), draws on much of this writing and contains an excellent bibliography.

2. The presence of dirk and dagger, firearms and bludgeons, in the records of college misdemeanors of the eighteenth and nineteenth centuries has been used to show the superior behavior of today's students. (See Wise, *ibid.*, pp. 33–35.) However, such comparisons usually take no account of the general changes in the conduct of the population over the same period of time. I doubt that the infrequency of shootings, knifings, and bloodshed on the modern campus says much about the college itself and its beneficial effect upon student behavior. After all, violence in Congress was more common in the nineteenth century than in the twentieth. The late Senator McCarthy was censured, not caned.
3. See Jerome Ellison, "Are We Making a Playground out of College?" *Saturday Evening Post,* Mar. 7, 1959.
4. Philip Jacob, *Changing Values in College* (New York: Harper, 1957), p. 3, "Except for the ritual of voting, they [the college students] are content to abdicate the citizen's role in the political process and to leave to others the effective power of governmental decision. They are politically irresponsible, and often politically illiterate as well." See also Ernest Havemann and Patricia West, *They Went to College* (New York: Harcourt, Brace, 1952), Chapter 10, "In the Voting Booth," pp. 108–125. "Indeed in the kind of activities that probably count the most, our graduates are all somewhat derelict. Only 17% had contributed money within the past year to a political cause or organization, and only 3% had done any fund-raising work for such a purpose. Moreover only 6% had held an elective office, or even unsuccessfully tried for one, within the past four years." P. 125.
5. At least two other incidents caused trouble last year. A State Representative in Oregon called the University of Oregon to account for permitting publication of "a ridiculous, vulgar, off-color piece of alleged literature" in *Facets,* a literary supplement of the student paper. In New Jersey, according to the *New York Times,* "An 18-year-old freshman at Rutgers University has become the target of attacks for a satirical poem on bigotry masked as patriotism. The poem was published recently in a campus magazine."
6. Wise, *op. cit.*, p. 42.
7. Robert H. Knapp and Joseph J. Greenbaum, *The Younger American Scholar: His Collegiate Origins* (Chicago: University of Chicago Press, 1953), p. 17.

Chapter 6: THE PLAYING FIELDS

1. Quoted in John Mooney, "Sports Mirror," *Salt Lake Tribune,* August 27, 1958, p. 21.
2. Howard J. Savage, *American College Athletics* (New York: Carnegie Foundation for the Advancement of Teaching, 1929), Bulletin No. 23, p. xxi.

3. The title and the sentence are not imaginary. The one came from *The Journal of Health-Physical Education-Welfare;* the other from *The Athletic Journal.*
4. Mooney, "Sports Mirror," May 20, 1959, p. 22.
5. Associated Press story, *Salt Lake Tribune,* Dec. 8, 1959, p. 24.
6. Mooney, "Sports Costs Crimp Colleges," *Salt Lake Tribune,* May 2, 1960, p. 20.
7. All quotations cited appeared in Mooney, "Sports Mirror," at various times: Grayson Kirk, May 20, 1959, p. 22; Alter, December 28, 1959, p. 25; Morrill, December 16, 1958, p. 20.
8. *Ohio State University Monthly,* LII (February, 1961), 17–32.

Chapter 7: THE BUREAUCRACY

1. H. Max Wise, *They Come for the Best of Reasons* (Washington: American Council on Education, 1958), pp. 1–4.
2. Hastings Rashdall, *The Universities in Europe in the Middle Ages* (Oxford, 1936), Vol. I, pp. 196–197.
3. Though this schedule is not an actual one, the courses are real and the schedule conforms to the pattern of first-year work in a majority of institutions.
4. Dietrich Gerhard, "The Emergence of the Credit System in American Education Considered as a Problem of Social and Intellectual History," *AAUP Bulletin,* XLI (Winter, 1955), 647–668.
5. *Ibid.,* p. 664.
6. Thorstein Veblen, *The Higher Learning in America* (New York: Sagamore Press, 1957), p. 93.
7. Robert M. Hutchins, *Freedom, Education, and the Fund* (New York: Meridian Books, 1956), p. 174.
8. *The College Presidency, 1900–1960, An Annotated Bibliography* (Washington: U.S. Government Printing Office, 1961), lists 700 separate publications pertaining to the subject.
9. Office of Education, Department of Health, Education and Welfare, "Highlights," *Faculty and Other Professional Staff in Institutions of Higher Education,* Circular No. 596, September, 1959.
10. *AAUP Bulletin,* XLII (Autumn, 1956), 559–560.
11. Dean E. McHenry, *The University of Nevada: An Appraisal* (Carson City, Nevada: Nevada Legislative Counsel Bureau, 1957), p. 44.

Chapter 8: THE FOURTH R

1. Martha Cox, "Remedial English: A Nation-Wide Survey," English Re-evaluation Committee, San Jose State College; "Has English Zero Seen Its Day?" *College Composition and Communication,* VIII (May, 1957), pp. 72–97. A survey of 76 major universities and state colleges made by San Jose State College in 1960 revealed that about half had discontinued or contemplated discontinuing the remedial English course. However, only five schools reported that students who failed to pass

the entrance or placement examination were refused admittance. These findings are supported by results of a survey taken by Office of Education which disclosed that one-fifth of colleges and universities had reduced the amount of subcollegiate instruction from 1954 to 1957. Office of Education, Department of Health, Education and Welfare, *College and University Faculties,* Bulletin 27 (Washington, 1959).

2. Bryson L. Jaynes, "Remedial English and College Graduation," *College Composition and Communication,* IX (February, 1958), 23–25; Lurene Brown, "A Look at Remedial English," *College English,* XVI (February, 1955), 303–305.
3. John T. Flautz, "The Complete Works in English of W——— G———," *College English,* XXI (April, 1961), 511–513. The whole essay is eminently worth reading. The examples of student writing could be matched by themes taken from almost any class in remedial English.
4. Harris W. Wilson, "Illinois vs. Illiteracy," *College Composition and Communication,* VII (May, 1956). As discussed in this report, cost is another reason for discontinuing remedial instruction.
5. Douglas Bush, "Education for All Is Education for None," *The New York Times Magazine,* January 9, 1955, p. 30. A closely reasoned, somewhat opposed view, is that of George Z. F. Bereday, "Intellect and Inequality in American Education," *The Educational Record,* XXXVII (July, 1958), 202–212.
6. "'Education for All Is Education for None,'" *The New York Times Magazine,* January 23, 1955, p. 63.
7. Byron S. Hollinshead, *Who Should Go to College* (New York: Columbia University Press, 1952), p. 123.
8. Ordway Tead, "The Problem of Equality in Higher Education," *The Journal of Higher Education,* XXVII (January, 1956), 6.
9. Tyrus Hillway, *The American Two-Year Junior College* (New York: Harper, 1958); James W. Thornton, Jr., *The Community Junior College* (New York: John Wiley & Sons, 1960); Office of Education, Department of Health, Education and Welfare, *The 2-Year Community College: An Annotated List of Studies and Surveys,* Bulletin 1958, No. 14 (Washington, 1958). Hillway gives the increase in junior colleges and enrollments as follows (the 1960 figure is from Thornton):

Date	Number of Jr. Colleges	Enrollment
1922	200	16,000
1950	600	500,000
1956–7	650	800,000
1960	677	905,062

10. It is understandable that the champions of the junior college movement do not want the junior college to be identified with students of low ability. Hillway, *op. cit.,* writes: "Even such an astute and well-informed observer of the American educational scene as James Bryant Conant seems to think of the two-year college primarily as an institution for students who do not have sufficient ability to 'make the grade' at reg-

ular four-year colleges. This is a basic misconception which might in the future do much harm to the development of junior and community college programs" (p. 84). My own hesitancy to accept the junior colleges as institutions for students of low ability is not so much because of the feelings of the junior colleges but because I do not think the junior colleges as they are now constituted have programs very well suited to the needs of students who find book learning difficult.

11. *Higher Education: Incentives and Obstacles* (Washington: American Council on Education, 1960), particularly John G. Darley, "Our Larger Purposes," pp. 17–32.

Chapter 9: Teaching

1. Malcolm Bradbury, "Can We Bring Back the Old-Fashioned Bank Robber?" *Harper's Magazine*, April, 1961, p. 38.
2. The best book on this precise subject is Gilbert Highet, *The Art of Teaching* (New York: Knopf, 1950).
3. John Q. Academesis (pseud.), *New York Times Magazine*, February 21, 1960, pp. 14, 72.
4. See Jessie L. Ward, "Promotional Factors in College Teaching," *The Journal of Higher Education*, VIII (1937), 475–479; Logan Wilson, *The Academic Man*, pp. 180–181; Office of Education, Federal Security Agency, *Toward Better College Teaching* (Washington: U. S. Government Printing Office, 1950).
5. Donald Lloyd, "Departmental Status Levels," *The CEA Critic*, XXII (October, 1960), 2–3.
6. Alfred North Whitehead, *The Aims of Education and Other Essays* (New York: Mentor Books, 1949), p. 102.

Chapter 10: Research

1. President's Science Advisory Committee, "Scientific Progress, the Universities, and the Federal Government," *Higher Education*, XVII (December, 1960), 5.
2. Jacques Barzun, "The Cults of 'Research' and 'Creativity,'" *Harper's Magazine*, October, 1960, pp. 70–71.
3. Examples from Charles Feidelson, Jr., and Paul Brodtkorb, Jr., eds., *Interpretations of American Literature* (New York: Galaxy Books, 1959).
4. John T. Flanagan, "Cold Light and Tumbling Clouds," *College English*, XXI (November, 1959), 86–89. Rebuttal, *College English*, XXI (April, 1960), 419–425.
5. John Gerber, "The Greater Struggle Necessary," *College English*, XVII (February, 1956), 249–250: "More recently our eagerness to appear scientific, especially in teaching the verbal skills, has become almost pathological."
6. Newman, *The Idea of a University* (Rinehart Editions 102, 1960), p. xl.
7. "Foreign language in Liberal Arts Education Today," *Publications of*

the Modern Language Association of America, XLVIII (June, 1953), xiii.

8. Dael Wolfle, *America's Resources of Specialized Talent* (New York: Harper, 1954), p. 33. The humanities and natural sciences have both lost ground to other fields since 1900. The humanities lost more ground, 1 graduate in 4 specializing in humanities in 1900 as compared with 1 in 8 now. Foreign languages lost most of all.
9. President's Science Advisory Committee, *op. cit.*, p. 4.

Chapter 11: MONEY

1. Harold Clark, *Life Earnings in Selected Occupations in the United States* (New York: Harper, 1937), p. 15.
2. John W. H. Walden, *The Universities of Ancient Greece* (New York, 1910), p. 191–192.
3. Educational Policies Commission, *Higher Education in a Decade of Decision* (Washington: National Education Association, 1957), pp. 123–127. Tables on gross national product and educational expenses taken from U.S. Department of Commerce and *Biennial Survey of Education* statistics. Figure on expenditures for tobacco in U.S. Department of Commerce, *Survey of Current Business*, XL (July, 1960): $7,034,000,000 in 1959. Estimated expenditure on higher education: $3,488,000,000 in 1960.
4. Office of Education, Department of Health, Education and Welfare, *Cost of Attending College*, Bulletin No. 9 (Washington: U.S. Government Printing Office, 1957).
5. Seymour Harris, "Broad Issues in Financing" in Dexter Keezer, *Financing Higher Education: 1960–70* (New York: McGraw-Hill, 1959), p. 63.
6. Henry S. Pritchett, "Preface," *The Financial Status of the Professor in America and in Germany* (New York: Carnegie Foundation for the Advancement of Teaching, 1908), (Bulletin No. 2), p. vi.
7. Committee on the Economic Status of the Profession, "Instructional Salaries in 41 Selected Colleges and Universities for the Academic Year 1955–56: Final Report," *AAUP Bulletin*, XLII (Spring, 1956), 30–31.
8. *Statistical Abstract of the United States 1961;* Office of Education, Department of Health, Education and Welfare, *Higher Education Planning and Management Data 1959–60*, Circular No. 614 (Washington: U.S. Government Printing Office, 1960).
9. Indirect testimony is to be found in Mary Jane Kaniuka, "A Summer Holiday in a College Town," *New York Times*, Section 10, June 25, 1961, which recommends a college campus as a place to visit or to vacation.
10. Lee DuBridge, "The Best Is None Too Good," *The Journal of Engineering Education*, XLIX (January, 1959), 306.
11. Keezer, *Financing Higher Education: 1960–70, op. cit.*, has a full discussion of many of the matters discussed in the conclusion of this chapter.
12. "Pricing and the Student Body," Part II, in Seymour E. Harris, ed.,

Higher Education in the United States: The Economic Problems (Cambridge, Mass.: Harvard University Press, 1960).

13. Robert D. Calkins, "Government Support of Higher Education" in Keezer, *Financing Higher Education: 1960–70, op. cit.*, pp. 183–219.
14. Educational Policies Commission, *Higher Education in a Decade of Decision, op. cit.*, p. 139; Keezer, *ibid.*, pp. 220–256, especially on corporate giving, p. 231.
15. Editorial "Big Enough Job for All," *Deseret News,* April 26, 1961, p. 18A.

Chapter 12: The Persistence of Problems

1. Abraham Flexner, *Universities: American, English, German* (New York: Oxford, 1930), p. 42.
2. "Faculty Council Minutes," University of Utah, Nov. 7, 1955 (multilithed).
3. The story is told in Gilbert Highet, *Man's Unconquerable Mind* (New York: Columbia University Press, 1954), pp. 19–20.
4. George Cram Cook, "The Third American Sex," *Forum,* L (1913), 445.
5. "Foreword," *The Upper Division in the College of Liberal Arts of Drake University: A Faculty Self Study* (Des Moines: Drake University, 1955) (multilithed).
6. Beardsley Ruml and Donald H. Morrison, *Memo to a College Trustee* (New York: McGraw-Hill, 1959), p. 61.
7. See Riesman, *Constraint and Variety in American Education* (Garden City: Doubleday Anchor Books, 1958), "The Intellectual Veto Groups," pp. 66–119, for a discussion of conflicting loyalties.
8. George B. Leonard, Jr., "Why Johnny Can't Write," *Look Magazine,* June 20, 1961, pp. 103–111.

Chapter 13: Achievements

1. For an excellent short history of higher education, see Richard Hofstadter and C. DeWitt Hardy, *The Development and Scope of Higher Education in the United States* (New York: Columbia University Press, 1952); the most comprehensive current history is John S. Brubacher and Willis Rudy, *Higher Education in Transition: An American History: 1636–1956* (New York: Harper, 1958).
2. *Basic Facts and Figures 1960* (UNESCO, 1961). The figure for England is based on university enrollment only. If the enrollment in technical and other vocational institutions were included—33,000 full-time, 218,000 part-time, and 700,000 evening students—the ratio would not be so startling.
3. The *New York Times Magazine* (August 20, 1961, pp. 16–17) reports that the number of students coming to American colleges and universities this fall is expected to surpass the record of 53,107 students from 143 countries at 166 institutions in 1960.
4. *Encyclopedia of Educational Research,* ed. by Walter S. Monroe, Rev.

Ed. (New York: Macmillan, 1956), pp. 1156–1158; Department of Labor, *Economic Forces in the U.S.A. in Facts and Figures*, 6th ed. (Washington: U.S. Government Printing Office, 1960), pp. 211–212.

5. Department of Labor, *op. cit.*, pp. 40–44.
6. Fraternities and sororities are far from moribund—there are 61 national fraternities with 3250 chapters in the United States and Canada and over 200,000 undergraduate members—but there is evidence that they mean much less than they once did. As a measure of the change in attitude, one might compare the well known article by Mrs. Glenn Frank, "Heartache on the Campus," published in *Woman's Home Companion*, April, 1945, with one by Stephen Birmingham, "Are Fraternities Necessary?" published in *Holiday*, October, 1958. Mrs. Frank's indignation rises out of the past: "The scars which fraternities and sororities deal out gratuitously to the thousands of students whom they turn down every year are reason enough alone, it seems to me, to condemn them to extinction, but they are guilty of other gross crimes against democracy." Mr. Birmingham's vague approval seems much closer to present student attitudes: "Fraternities, whether taken seriously or not, seem to fill some sort of gap in college life." It seems clear to me that then, or now, they fill it badly. A middle point of view and that of a college president can be found in Kenneth I. Brown, "Salt on a College Campus," *Journal of Higher Education*, XXI (February, 1950), 57–65.
7. Edward Eddy, *The College Influence on Student Character* (Washington: American Council on Education, 1959), pp. 158–159.
8. Baker Brownell, *The College and the Community* (New York: Harper, 1952).
9. *The University and World Affairs* (New York: The Ford Foundation, 1960), p. 3.
10. George Santayana, *Character and Opinion in the United States* (New York: George Braziller, 1955); especially "Materialism and Idealism in American Life," pp. 93–108.
11. Charles Frankel, ed., *The Uses of Philosophy, An Irwin Edman Reader* (New York: Simon and Schuster, 1955), p. 106.
12. The conclusions about the veterans and idealism are admittedly subjective. Studies seem to show that as a group the veterans were strongly drawn to vocational training, particularly to engineering and business. However, most academic observers of veterans on campus have spoken of the veteran's stronger sense of purpose, his impatience with campus frivolity, and his somewhat better performance over the nonveteran student. *Time*, reviewing the program (August 6, 1956), pointed out that it had produced 238,000 teachers, 180,000 doctors and nurses, 113,000 scientists, 107,000 lawyers, and 36,000 clergymen. For a brief, thoughtful discussion of the veterans' impact on the colleges, see Ernest Earnest, *Academic Procession: An Informal History of the American College (1636–1953)* (Indianapolis-New York: Bobbs-Merrill, 1953), pp. 320–324.

Chapter 14: Drive Versus Drift

1. See Special Studies Project, Report V, Rockefeller Brothers Fund, Inc., *The Pursuit of Excellence* (Garden City, N.Y.: Doubleday, 1958), and the expansion of that report in John W. Gardner, *Excellence* (New York: Harper, 1961).
2. Dael Wolfle, *America's Resources of Specialized Talent* (New York, Harper, 1954), p. 181.
3. T. C. Holy, "California's Master Plan for Higher Education, 1960–1975," *Journal of Higher Education*, XXXII (January, 1961), 9–16.
4. Compact information about these programs is available in the "New Dimensions in Higher Education" series of the U.S. Office of Education. See pamphlets No. 1, "Independent Study"; No. 7, "Quest for Quality"; and No. 8, "Advanced Standing."
5. See Office of Education, Department of Health, Education and Welfare, *Advanced Standing* (Washington: New Dimensions in Higher Education series, No. 8, 1961), for an outline of this and similar programs.
6. David Riesman in *Higher Education in the United States: The Economic Problems* (Cambridge, Mass.: Harvard University Press, 1960), pp. 174, 175.
7. Ruth E. Eckert, "Who Teach in Departments and Schools of Education?" *The Journal of Teacher Education*, X (December, 1959), 497–502. This study of Minnesota colleges reaches conclusions similar to those reached in earlier studies. Faculty in schools or departments of education differ from the rest of the faculty in crucial ways: fewer enter the profession as a result of planning, early or late, to become college teachers; fewer win undergraduate honors, graduate awards, or earned doctorates; fewer engage in research as part of their professional life; fewer men staff college of education faculties; and more are graduates of teachers colleges.
8. The adverse developments anticipated here and other changes taking place in the liberal arts college are discussed forcefully in two pamphlets by Earl J. McGrath, *Are Liberal Arts Colleges Becoming Professional Schools?* and *The Graduate School and the Decline of Liberal Education* (New York: Teachers College, Columbia University, 1958 and 1959).

Chapter 15: Hopes and Proposals

1. Fred M. Hechinger, "Case History of an Academic Prodigy," *New York Times Magazine*, June 4, 1961, p. 12.
2. C. L. Barber, Donald Sheehan, Stuart M. Stoke, Shannon McCune, *The New College Plan: A Proposal for a Major Departure in Higher Education* (Amherst, Mass.: University of Massachusetts, 1958).
3. Shannon McCune, "The New College Plan," in Seymour Harris, ed., *Higher Education in the United States: The Economic Problems* (Cam-

bridge, Mass.: Harvard University Press, 1960), p. 141. See also Part V, "Experiments in Higher Education," in this volume for discussion of other experiments, and Pamphlets No. 3, "The Experimental College," and No. 7, "The Quest for Quality," in the "New Dimensions in Higher Education" series.

4. See Brubacher and Rudy, *Higher Education in Transition* (New York: Harper, 1958), Chapter 11, "The Federal Government and Higher Education," pp. 216–22, for discussion of repeated attempts to establish a national university.
5. Everett C. Hughes, "Non-Economic Aspects of Academic Morale," in *Higher Education in the United States: The Economic Problems, op. cit.*, p. 118.
6. Lotus D. Coffman, *The State University: Its Work and Problems* (Minneapolis: University of Minnesota Press, 1934), p. 130.
7. "The Claremont colleges": See E. Wilson Lyon, "English Precedents in the Associated Colleges at Claremont," *Association of American Colleges Bulletin*, XXXIV (October, 1948), 270–275.
8. Gilbert Highet, "Teaching, Not Facts, But How to Think," *New York Times Magazine*, February 25, 1951, p. 44.